Optimize Quality for Business Outcomes

A Practical Approach to Software Testing

Andreas Golze
Charlie Li
Shel Prince

A Mercury Press Publication

379 North Whisman Road, Mountain View, CA 94043

ISBN-10: 0-615-13383-5

ISBN-13: 978-0-615-13383-6

First Edition

Edited by Beverly Hanly

Contents

Acknowledgements

Without the help from many fine people, this book would not have been possible. We'd like to thank those who have contributed ideas and those who have shaped our thoughts and concepts over the years.

Help and encouragement has come from many departments within Mercury, as well as from friends and colleagues outside the company. Mercury departments lending a hand include Professional Services, R&D, Marketing, and Product Marketing.

While naming individuals risks inadvertently leaving out some names, we would be remiss if we failed to mention the following people:

Murat Aksu, Onagh Ash, Arya Barirani, Heinz Bons, Pete Chargin, Ariel Cohen, Ray Ffrench, Zohar Gilad, Dione Hedgpeth, Ed Kit, Youhua Li, Zheng Li, Marcy Mills, Matt Morgan, Greg Pope, Rajesh Radhakrishnan, Jonathan Rende, Ted Sfikas, Imran Tusneem, and Valerie Weager. We did not realize what it takes to put a book together and we've learned a lot from the Oak Hill team, so thanks to Bev, Mira, Greg, Amy, Linda, and Faith.

We especially want to thank our spouses, **Petra Harren**, **Mandy Mobley Li**, and **Nancy Prince**, for putting up with our insanely long work hours and the incessant traveling. And **Patrick**, **Leif**, **Thekla**, and **Cedric**, thanks for doing so often without your dad. Without our families' support, this book certainly would not have happened.

Andreas Golze

Charlie Li

Shel Prince

Introduction

The word *testing* has many meanings. Teachers test their students to see how much they've learned, small children test the taste and feel of almost anything by putting things in their mouths, and scientists test the strength of materials to see how far they can be stressed before they break. (Some people say teenagers do the same thing to their parents!)

But those kinds of testing are not what we discuss in this book. Software testing is a process where we check a behavior we observe against a specified behavior the business expects.

The trial-and-error behavior that helps us learn and understand the world as children is testing without understanding the expected result.

Both methods of testing have elements in common. In both methods, we want to find out what happens if we're using something in a specific way. The primary difference is that in software testing, the tester should know what behavior to expect as defined by the business requirements. We agree on this defined, expected behavior and any user can observe this behavior.

Today, we see folks in the IT industry still confusing these two concepts of testing. Often, two groups of people are doing software testing:

- The developers or engineers who build the software application want to make sure the final product works as they intended. The testing is done from an IT or technical perspective without relating back to the business.
- The end users who will be using the final product in their jobs, in many cases, do ad-hoc testing based on their day-to-day work experience. They make assumptions of how the application should work that come from their individual needs and ideas. Their approach is more trial and error than systemized testing — it's often ineffective and creates a lot of rework.

If each group is testing based on their needs and ideas, who's testing for the business outcomes? Who validates that the application will meet business requirements? Who mitigates the risk of failure of a software application in production?

Software testing, like software development, is a profession. Testers need to master proven techniques. Organizations like the British Computer Society and the International Software Testing Qualifications Board (ISTQB) have begun building standardized training and granting testing certification levels.

Like developers, software testers are a special breed with unique talents that can bridge the gap between the business and IT. They must have technical skills coupled with a business mentality. To build a professional test team and do testing with rigor, not by trial and error, takes time and money. For most companies using IT as the backbone for their business, time and money are the two things that are not readily available.

We, along with our colleagues, have consulted with thousands of customers on quality and testing and have seen the same issues time after time. In this book, we present a pragmatic solution to help address some of these challenges.

Our goal is not to write a comprehensive book on testing or advanced testing theory. We're showing you practical solutions, based on implementation experience. If we can help organizations solve some of their most important quality challenges quickly, we have succeeded in what we've set out to achieve here.

In this book, we address fundamental questions around testing from a business perspective.

- In Chapter 1, we examine why testing is so important to a successful product launch.
- In Chapter 2, we discuss how we know what to test and how to determine that testing has met its objectives.
- In Chapters 3 and 4, we present efficient, effective methods of software test design called behavioral modeling.
- In Chapter 5, we define practical implementation strategies for optimizing software testing, as well as show how to prioritize testing tasks and which parts of testing should be automated.
- In Chapter 6, we give you a *SUCCESSFUL* approach to measuring and using key performance indicators.
- In Chapter 7, we offer some guidance on how to start implementing the concepts in this book.
- The appendices contain technical details, tips, tricks, and guidelines for those who want to go further with these concepts and begin to implement them.

Throughout this book, we use the phrase *business function(s)* to define a set of discrete end-user steps that constitute a basic business activity such as "log in," "search for a flight," or "register user." In some application environments the terms, *process steps* or *work steps* may be used instead.

We hope you gain a new business perspective on software testing and find some practical guidance for implementing quality improvements within your organization.

We might say, "Enjoy!" But we know what you'll really enjoy is the confidence that you know how to move through your software development cycle in the most efficient, cost-effective way — and that you know your customers will be satisfied at the end of it. We will share this win-win process with you.

Chapter 1

What Is the Big Deal About Testing?

"For want of a nail, the shoe was lost.
For want of a shoe, the horse was lost.
For want of a horse, the rider was lost.
For want of a rider, the battle was lost.
For want of a battle the kingdom was lost.
And all for the want of a horseshoe nail."
(traditional)

We at Mercury, along with our colleagues, have several thousand man years of experience in quality management and software testing, and we've learned that proper testing can help a business save a significant amount of money on product development, reduce time to market, and gain satisfied customers.

Finding defects early in the development process makes for a product development cycle that satisfies both the business stakeholders and the customers — we can vouch for that.

In manufacturing, for instance, a perfect example of the approach we favor is Toyota's. In a huge departure from the hallowed big four U.S. automakers, Toyota aligned its business requirements with its users.

- They test a cup holder like a user would, not like a designer.
- Any person on the manufacturing floor can stop the entire manufacturing process if they notice something is not right.
- Everybody on the assembly line is a quality checker.
- When a problem is spotted early, it's a lot cheaper to fix at that point, instead of cranking out a bunch of flawed cars and later having to rework the design, or possibly even do a recall.

The Mercury Quality Model was born out of our customers' question, "How can we save IT costs for testing and quality management?"

To find the answer, we followed the approach made popular by Taiichi Ohno, inventor of the Toyota Quality System, and others. The 5-Why method asks five questions that help lead us down the right path.

First, we asked: **Why is IT so expensive, when hardware costs are dropping and development technologies have improved developer productivity?**

We found that despite the advancements in IT process and technology, IT projects are becoming more complex and they almost always run out of time. When time is short, people tend to sacrifice the quality of the product.

The Standish Report over the past 15 years shows the rate of successful projects (that is, under budget and on time) is below 30 percent (Figure 1). The advancements haven't lowered the cost. On the contrary, with more complexity, the need for proper planning and project management is greater.

When budget and time constraints dictate the project parameters, functionality and quality get the short end of the stick.

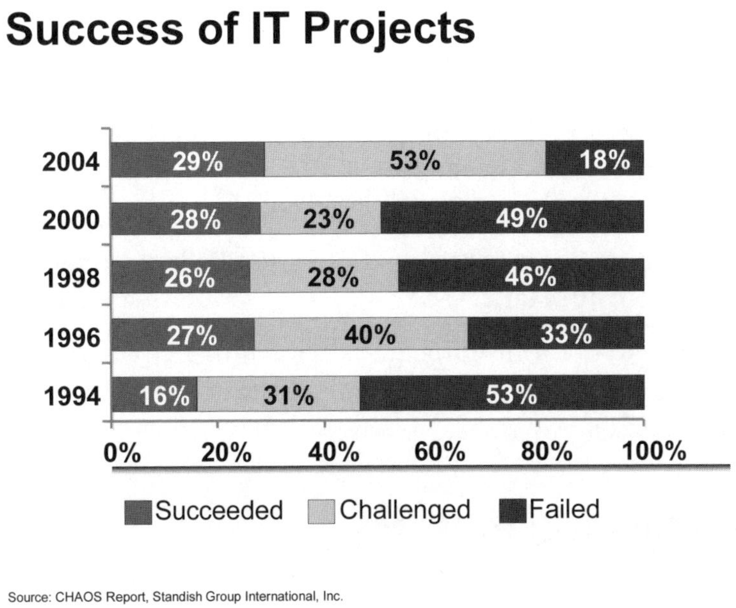

Figure 1: IT project success-rate status has changed over the past 10 years

To learn why the success rate is so low, we wondered: **Why were the successful projects successful?**

The Standish group also collected data on success factors, asking respondents what contributed to their project's success. Executive support and user involvement were high on the list. Here are the other factors that figured in project success.

- Executive support (18%)
- User involvement (16%)
- Experienced project manager (14%)
- Clear business objectives (12%)
- Minimized scope (10%)
- Standard software infrastructure (8%)
- Firm basic requirements (6%)

- Reliable estimates (5%)
- Other criteria (5%)

While we expected to see executive support and experienced project management, we were interested in other noteworthy elements like user involvement, clear business objectives, and firm basic requirements on the list.

All three of those factors have to do with the end user or the business, which leads us to the next question: **Why is user involvement so important?**

The answer lies in the following statistics (Figure 2), based on a 2002 study conducted by the National Institute of Science and Technology (NIST).

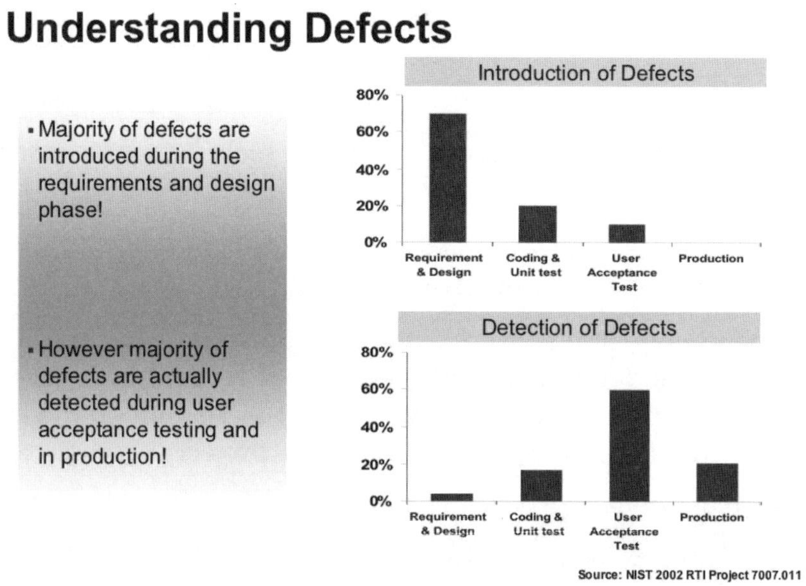

Figure 2: Comparison of where defects are introduced against where they are discovered

Figure 2 shows that most defects are introduced in the requirements phase of the traditional software development life cycle (SDLC).

> Defects in this phase happen mostly because the requirements themselves are incomplete, ambiguous, or contradictory.

When unclear requirements are translated into developers' technical specifications, misalignment of the original ambiguous business requirement and misinterpreted technical specification results in significant rework. (Interestingly, the same people who created the requirements and introduced problems in the requirements phase couldn't see their mistakes until the user acceptance phase, when they could spot them.)

So, we recommend as a best practice for those creating requirements — double-check initial requirements for ambiguity, contradictions, and incompleteness.

This effect is not limited to software. The following example shows what can happen in situations where people omit necessary details — they have a clear idea of what they want and have made preconceived assumptions, but neglect to communicate the specifics of what they require.

The whole process begins when somebody needs something — in this case a means of transport (the product) — and expresses an expectation (the requirement).

The contractor asks no questions because he has a picture in his mind of what the customer wants. Now, the contractor has made an assumption without checking with the customer. We're clearly missing some communication — a requirement proof point here.

The building process starts and soon, the contractor hands the product over to the customer for acceptance.

During the acceptance phase, the customer rejects the product because important features are missing, and more requirements are added. Instead of starting from scratch, the developer tries to incorporate the new features into the existing construction.

At this point, people rarely go back to their initial assumption (in this case, that the customer needs a bicycle) to find out whether the additional information (the customer doesn't want to get wet and needs to carry a briefcase) means the whole design should be reconsidered.

The reason seems to be that we make decisions based on our own perspective of the situation, rather than use a mechanism that would help obtain a more complete picture. As a result, we attempt to solve the problem without solving the problem.

Despite all efforts to the contrary, we've got an unhappy customer along with a wasted investment into something that doesn't solve the problem.

After more iterations, the solution the contractor comes up with will be more what the customer originally wanted and the problem is solved. But taking the time to sort that out in today's dynamic marketplace means we have compromised:

- Time to market
- Cost efficiency
- Efficiency of the solution

Applying this common example to the concepts of software development, we come to the next question: **Why is the late discovery of defects a major concern, as long as defects are detected and fixed?**

The answer lies in the cost of fixing defects in various stages of the SDLC (Figure 3).

Assessing Cost of Defects

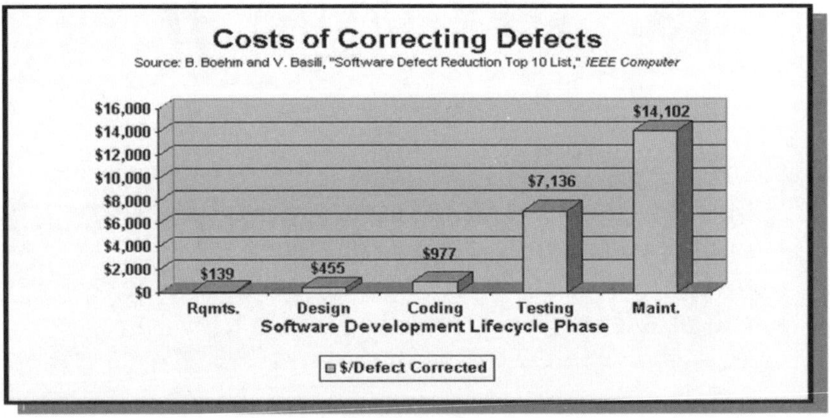

This industry average is used as a baseline for arriving at cost savings

Industry References: B. Boehm and V. Basili, "Software Defect Reduction Top 10 List, " IEEE Computer, IEEE Computer Society, Vol. 34, No. 1, January 2001, pp. 135-137.

Figure 3: The cost of correcting defects increases dramatically as we move toward the end of the SDLC

If we are complacent, neglecting to identify defects introduced in the requirements phase until we get to User Acceptance Testing, we lose approximately $7,000 per defect. This quickly adds up to significant numbers. It also results in the failure of many IT projects when most of the budget for the project is already spent and a huge additional monetary outlay is needed toward the end of the project.

In our bicycle/car example, all the extra work and investment was for something essentially useless to the business. In a business situation, if we consider other indirect costs that crop up, from added time-to-market and increased project risk, the cost can really break a business.

This leads to the final question: **Why can't we make use of this knowledge to improve the testing process?**

To answer that question let's first look at some testing definitions:

> Testing is about finding defects, bugs, or flaws.

This is true for software, as well as for all other products built to suit specific needs. Testing is done by everyone all the time, so why bother?

If we start looking at the testing process more carefully, we find that in most cases, testing is not just about finding defects, but also about knowing whether a product meets business expectations.

> Testing is to determine if a product meets business expectations.

Although this sounds pretty much the same, there is a fundamental difference. A defect is any flaw or imperfection in a software product or process. This implies that a definition of the perfect working product has been made and is clear to all stakeholders. It's not a defect just because the expectations of an individual tester have not been met.

Unfortunately, intuitive testing based on undocumented expectations is a common approach in the industry today. This testing approach is limited because it only works with the completed product and does not allow testing to be done early enough in the software development life cycle or in parallel with development.

The answer to the last question is that we can't improve the testing process using this knowledge because in today's market, IT often dominates discussions around product expectations and defines the desired functionality around technological aspects rather than business needs. Therefore, the testing process is often misaligned with the needs of the business or ideal business outcomes.

> The Mercury Quality Model is a pragmatic approach to software testing that aligns IT with business outcomes.

Quality Goals and Test Stages

To build meaningful and concise tests, we need to define requirements that describe the system behavior we anticipate. But that alone would not be enough to specify the intensity or the coverage needed for the tests to meet the end users' quality goals.

Quality goals are nonfunctional requirements. Typically in IT projects, we use these quality goals:

- **Adaptability** — How easily software can be modified to meet new requirements.
- **Maintainability** — How easily a component can be modified to correct faults, improve performance or other attributes, or adapt to a changed environment.
- **Modularity** — How much of a system or computer program is composed of discrete components and a

change to one component has minimal impact on other components.

- **Generality** — The breadth of applicability of the component.
- **Portability** — How easily a system or component can be transferred from one hardware or software environment to another.
- **Reliability** — The ability of a component to perform its required functions under stated conditions for a specified period of time.
- **Correctness** — How free a component is from faults in its specification, design, and implementation. It is also how well a component meets specified requirements or user needs and expectations. And, it's the ability of a component to produce specified outputs when given specified inputs, and the extent to which they match or satisfy the requirements.
- **Completeness** — How well the component implements all required capabilities.
- **Efficiency** — How well a component performs its designated functions using minimal resources.
- **Understandability** — How clear the meaning of a software component is to the user.
- **Performance** — How well the article under test (AUT) meets the performance needs of the user. Performance may be a measure of throughput, response time, transaction or data volume, or any other related measure.

Obviously it is not possible to test against all the different goals in one step. So testing is usually conducted using test stages in a phased approach. Each test stage concentrates on stage-specific quality goals and requires a different level of readiness of the product.

This phased approach is a common practice in engineering and is done to assure the quality of a single unit, before it is verified as an integrated unit to other units. The positive effects are obvious:

- When you discover an error before getting too far down the production line, it pays off in tremendous cost savings.
- It's easy to troubleshoot a product or process, or do root-cause analysis, when each element has been tested. (For instance, if you're building a brick wall, each brick has been tested before being placed in the wall so you know the problem is in the wall structure — you don't have to test the bricks again.)
- You enter every integration step with a known quality of the components (the bricks).
- Testing is easier because the functionality to be tested is limited to the component to be tested.

The test stages build on each other and are defined in such a way that testing can be done as early as possible in the software development life cycle. Because cost efficiency is crucial, it typically does not make sense to enter a test stage before the previous stage has met its exit criteria. For example, it may not be effective to do performance testing before unit testing is complete.

The prerequisite for each test stage is that the preceding test stage was executed successfully to a certain extent. The entry and exit criteria used for each test stage are called Quality Gates. They are introduced at the beginning and end of each phase and determine the success of the test stages.

In the Mercury Quality Model, we recommend the following test phases:

Requirements Verification

In the Requirements Verification phase, the end user adds acceptance criteria to each requirement in order to answer the question, "What would make me sign off on this requirement?" The acceptance criteria needs to:

- Validate the completeness and correctness of the requirements.
- Associate the requirements with the business functions.
- Eliminate ambiguities.
- Validate that the result of each requirement is testable.
- Identify the business functions that are changed during this project (maintenance projects only).

Unit Test

The Unit Test is a white-box test conducted by the developers to find out whether the application is stable and completely implemented from a developer's perspective. (We look into white-box and black-box testing later in this chapter.)

Unit testing validates that a particular module of source code is working as the developer intended. A developer conducts the testing, not an end user. A unit has to be executable and the developer uses a debugger or self-developed tools to find out whether the code meets his expectations and the technical specification.

Integration Test

The Integration Test phase has two stages:

- **Business Function Test** — Business function testing is the first black-box test phase where the functionality of each business function is tested against the requirements.
- **Business Process Test** — Business process testing checks the business process end-to-end inside the application and focuses on the correct implementation of the interfaces between the business functions.

System Test

The System Test is conducted on a complete, integrated system to evaluate the entire system's compliance with its specified business requirements. System testing falls within the scope of black-box testing, and as such, should require no knowledge of the inner design of the code or logic.

Performance Test

The Performance Test determines the performance and scalability of some aspect of a system — how it performs under a real-world workload. This test may measure throughput, volume limits, transaction time, or any other similar metrics.

User Acceptance Test

The User Acceptance Test (UAT) is done by users or their representatives on a new or changed information system. If the system behaves according to their expectations, the user acceptance testers approve deploying the system. Cosmetic and other small changes may still be required as a result of the test, but the system is considered stable and behaving according to requirements.

Operational Readiness Test

The Operational Readiness Test is the final phase of testing performed on the prospective production system. This test is scheduled and conducted as a part of the production go-live plan. It is to be executed after all other cutover activities are complete, and prior to any go/no-go considerations. The Operational Readiness Test Summary Report is the final business acceptance signoff.

Each test stage requires a particular completeness of the components to be tested. These components have to be executed in a certain sequence, which is synchronized with the progress of the development team. The test stages are repeated for every release of the software and they define the software test life cycle — a parallel process with the software development life cycle, but the two are also integrated (Figure 4).

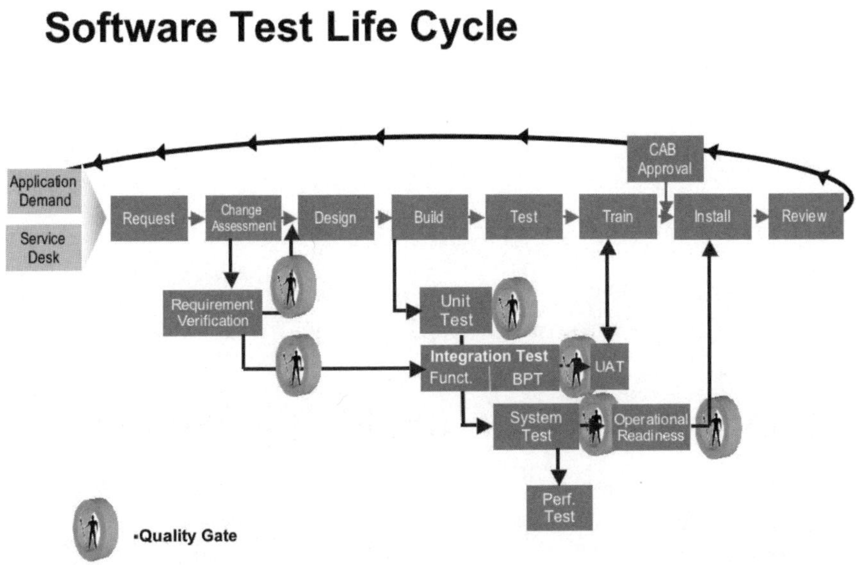

Figure 4: The software test life cycle is shown running parallel to and integrated with the SDLC.

Case Study: Flight Application

We'll illustrate how the phased approach is applied by examining the operation of a web-based portal that allows customers to book airline flights.

The portal is an easy-to-use, straightforward solution that allows customers to search, select, and book flights in the flight database. The system interfaces with the centralized booking system based on the Systems, Applications, and Products in the Data Processing (enterprise resource planning [ERP]) financial module.

Customers have to register before they can use the system. The customer-related information is stored in the centralized customer relationship manager (CRM) system, along with users' passwords. The following functions are needed:

- Log on
- Log off
- Register
- Search flight
- Book flight

Requirements Verification

The prerequisite for the Requirements Verification is broken down into logical business functions (Figure 5).

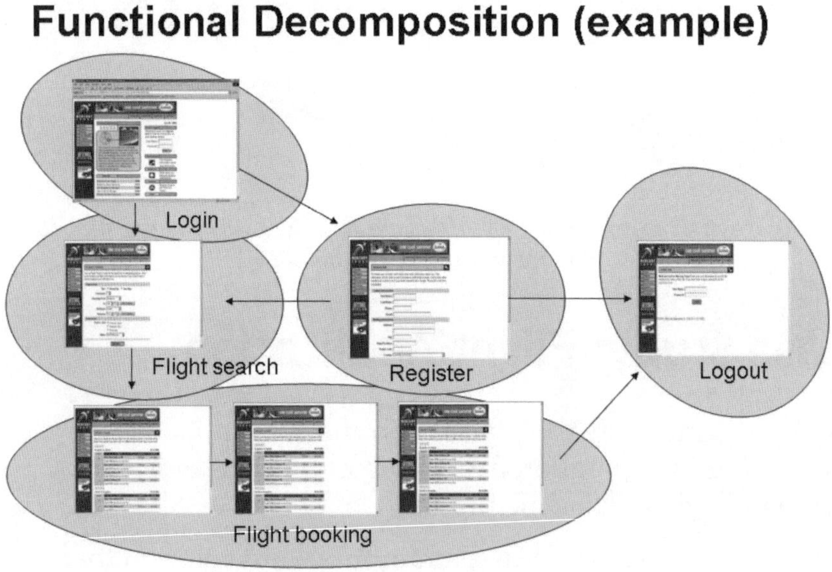

Figure 5: The business process is broken down into business functions

Requirements Verification documents the acceptance criteria for each requirement of each separate business function.

Suppose one requirement for the business function LOG IN is: "The user has to enter a username and a password. By pressing a <LOG IN> button or ENTER on the keyboard, the validation of username and password should start."

Then acceptance criteria for that requirement could be:

- If a username without a password is entered, an error message is displayed.
- If the username and the password are a correct combination, the system shows the flight-search screen.
- If the username and the password are not a valid combination, an error message is displayed.

Ideally, the business analyst or business user writing the acceptance criteria identifies missing information and ambiguities in the requirements, documents those as defects, and hands them over to the development team.

Possible quality gates for the Requirements Verification Test are:

- One hundred percent of the requirements have at least one documented acceptance criterion (such as the online flight booking).
- We have divided the application into business functions and prioritized each business function according to the quality needed to meet the business goal of allowing the user to book a flight online.

Unit Test

Unit testing is part of the development life cycle, so we don't make specific recommendations for this phase in our airline booking example.

However, we need to agree on the quality gates for the Unit Test, because it defines the quality level we can expect when the software is handed over. In other words, if the software does not meet the defined criteria, the test team will not accept it for the Integration Test.

Possible quality gates for the Unit Test are:

- **Statement Coverage** — Has each line of the source code been executed and tested?
- **Condition Coverage** — Has each evaluation point (such as a true/false decision) been executed and tested?
- **Path Coverage** — Has every possible route through a given part of the code been executed and tested?

Integration Test

During the Integration Test we first look at the implementation of each business function. After we validate that the business function is functioning correctly, we can move to the next phase, the various combinations of business functions.

Business Function Test

We're testing these business functions in our example applications:

- Log on
- Log off
- Register
- Flight search
- Flight booking

We test each function independently as soon as it has passed the Unit Test, using various approaches to complete the function test. We suggest using behavioral modeling for the test case development (we'll explain more in Chapters 4 and 5).

Regardless of the applied methodology, the quality gates need to be defined and met.

Possible quality gates for the Business Function Test are:

- All planned test cases have been executed.
- All incidents have been logged as defects.

- All identified defects have been resolved. ("Resolved" means they're either closed or a decision has been made to delay the closing.)

Business Process Test

When it comes to the Business Process Test, we want to make sure to test the various possible business function sequences. In our flight-booking example, the possible process is shown in Figure 6.

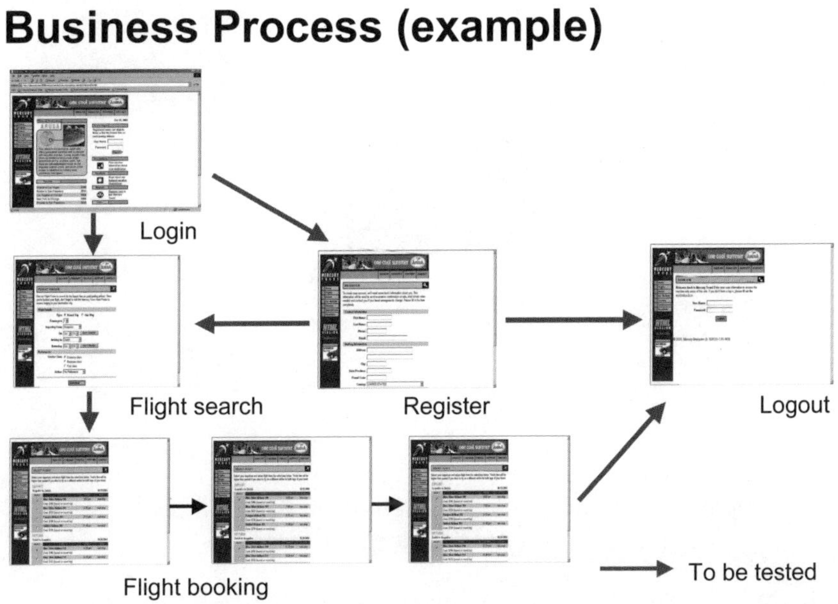

Figure 6: Sample business process for a flights application

It's important to test each possible connection between the business functions once. The focus is the transition from one business function to the next and not the functional correctness of the single business function (addressed during the Business Function Test).

Possible quality gates for the Business Process Test might be:

- All end-to-end processes can be executed.
- A workaround exists for all defects found.

System Test

During the System Test, each individual application should have passed the quality gates for the integration test. The System Test often involves large and complex environments with multiple independent applications working together to support a business process (Figure 7).

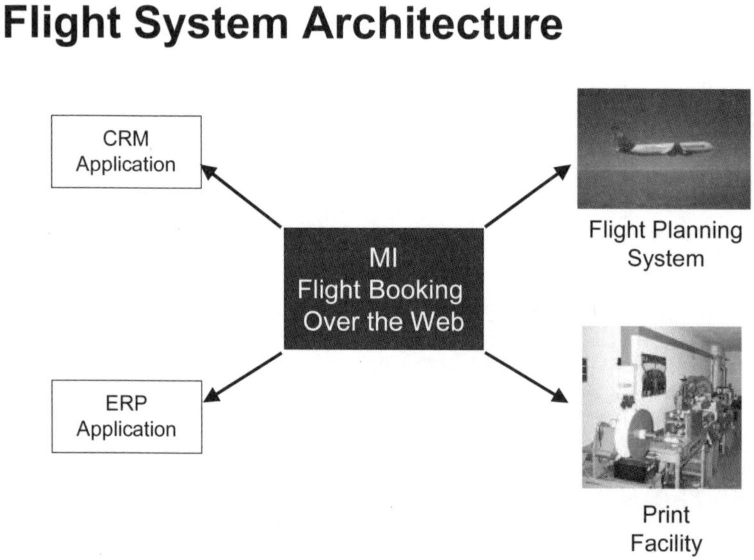

Figure 7: A flight-booking system is supported by multiple independent applications

The System Test makes sure various applications work together as the business process requires — flight planning, ticketing, customer relations. The focus of the system test is:

- **Functional correctness** — All interfacing applications are in place and the application functions correctly in the defined environment.
- **Usability** — The product can be employed by users to achieve specified goals effectively and efficiently in a specified context of use.

- **Reliability** — The system can perform and maintain its functions in routine circumstances, as well as in hostile or unexpected circumstances.
- **Accessibility** — A system is usable by as many people as possible with modification.

Possible quality gates for the System Test are:

- All end-to-end processes can be executed.
- No severe defects exist.

Performance Test

The Performance Test helps us:

- Demonstrate that the system meets performance criteria.
- Compare two systems to find which performs better.
- Measure which parts of the system or workload cause the system to perform badly.

When troubleshooting, software engineers use tools such as profilers to measure which parts of a device or software contribute most to the poor performance or to establish throughput levels (and thresholds) to maintain acceptable response time.

> The later a performance defect is detected, the higher the cost of remediation.

When Performance testing begins at the inception of the development project and extends through to deployment, you have a better chance of catching defects early and thereby saving money and time that would otherwise have to be budgeted to fix problems down the line. This is true in the case of Functional testing, but even more so with Performance testing, because of the end-to-end nature of its scope.

In Performance testing, it is crucial (but often difficult to arrange) for the test conditions to be similar to the expected actual use.

In our example, the Performance Test would follow the schema shown in Figure 8.

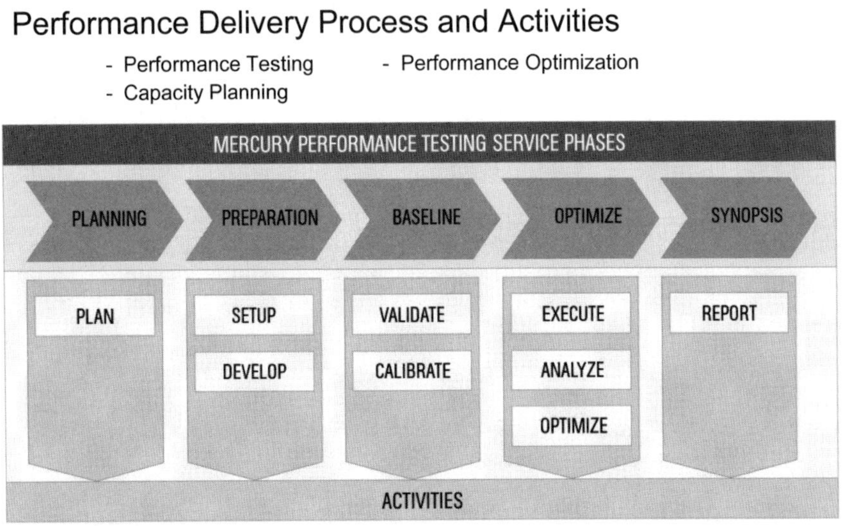

Figure 8: We recommend this Performance-testing delivery model

During the planning phase it's important to define an end-user behavior scenario that's as close as possible to the real behavior you expect from a user. This has to be done for the number of users, as well as for the transactions they perform using the application.

Possible quality gates for the Performance Test, which are derived from the performance requirements, are:

- The volume and rate of end-user activity
- End-user transaction response time(s)
- End-user transaction error rate
- Server uptime and utilization measurements

User Acceptance Test

When users are satisfied that the business functional specifications and business requirements have been met, system sign-off and release can take place. The User Acceptance Test (UAT) phase involves turning loose a number of real end users to try the system, using it as they would in real life to accomplish whatever task the system is designed for.

The goal is to make sure that the end users are comfortable with the system they will be working with and that all their requirements are met.

Often a team will leverage training of the end users as a means to perform user acceptance testing. In our flight example, we might have reservation agents go through the system and make flight reservations and help identify any issues in the flight system.

The quality gate for the UAT is the end-user sign-off.

Operational Readiness Test

The project requirements and design specification documents clearly define the expectations for systems operational readiness. We've been aware of operational readiness levels while we've conducted previous testing phases (Unit, System, Integration, Performance, and UAT).

Operational Readiness testing ensures that the system we are about to deliver has the appropriate production data loaded, is ready to communicate with required external systems, and is ready to run the necessary regular batch processes, while meeting any specific security and compliance requirements.

For the flight application, we might check to make sure that the flight data is being populated correctly, that billing processes that use an external system are working, and that the ticket purchase process is done through secure channels so users are not worried about sharing their private information.

This test stage is the last check of the production system for operational readiness before the system go-live point. This stage should be a part of the Project Implementation Plan.

Key elements of operational readiness testing are:

- End-user setup
- Role definitions and requirements
- Security allocations and passwords
- End-to-end connectivity verification
- Production data verification
- Core business functionality verification
- Removable or read-only system interaction
- Application monitoring tool verification
- Call/Service center support setup
- Support documentation

The quality gates for operational readiness are normally defined by the operations team or, if the operations task is outsourced, these quality gates can be defined by a combination of the service providers that host the application and the internal operations team.

Test Concepts and Techniques

Many test techniques have been developed over the years for the different test stages but there are two basic types of test: The white-box test and the black-box test.

White-Box Testing

White-box testing is also known as clear-box testing, glass-box testing, or structural testing. The term *white box* (or glass box) indicates that the tester knows the code used to execute certain functionality.

In software testing, it's usually a programmer that performs white-box tests. Often, multiple programmers will write tests based on certain code to gain various perspectives on possible outcomes.

In the fields of computer programming, software engineering, and software testing, white-box testing is used to check that the outputs of a program, given certain inputs, conform to the structural specifications of the program. In electrical hardware testing, every node in a circuit may be probed and measured (in-circuit test, or ICT).

The most common techniques and approaches used in white-box testing are syntax testing, statement testing, branch/decision testing, data flow testing, branch condition testing, branch condition combination testing, and modified condition decision testing. (For detailed descriptions of these test techniques, see Appendix A.)

Black-Box Testing

In white-box testing we saw that the tester — usually the developer — had insight into how the application was developed. However, when a third party or impartial tester does not know how the programs were developed, they can conduct black-box testing.

In computer programming, software engineering, and software testing, we use black-box testing (also known as concrete box or functional testing) to check that the outputs of a program, given certain inputs, conform to the functional specification of the program. In electrical hardware testing, we black-box test the specifications of the interface between the device and application circuit.

The term *black box* indicates that the tester does not examine the internal implementation of the program being executed. For this reason, black-box testing is not normally carried out by the programmer. In most engineering firms, one group does design work and a separate group does the testing.

The most common techniques and approaches used in black-box testing are the smoke test, equivalence partitioning, boundary value analysis, and user input validation. (For detailed descriptions of these tests techniques, see Appendix A.)

Wrapping Up

By now, you can see how testing can help your company's bottom line in a new product release, saving you considerable money by catching flaws early in the process and reducing rework for your team.

We've showed you how our approach works in the software field, but you can apply this method in most any industry and it's an excellent way to troubleshoot internal business processes.

> By setting out clear requirements that align with your business goals, you'll save yourself some headaches and preserve good customer relations.

Our experiences with other test methodologies have led us to adopt an approach to test design that departs somewhat from traditional testing. It's aligned with business outcomes and is focused on the end-user experience — testing to make sure the customer will have a satisfactory experience, not just that developers see the results they expect.

But before we start testing, we have to better understand what to test.

Chapter 2

Testing the Business Requirements: Start at the Root of the Problem

The Mercury Quality Model (MQM) attacks the primary source of application defects: requirements. According to the United States National Institute of Standards and Technology, incomplete, vague, or conflicting requirements typically cause a whopping 70 percent of an application's defects.

Using our structured approach to testing the requirements, you can find and correct these problems before development — or even design — begins.

> Clear requirements improve the final quality, reduce time to complete the project and lower the cost of project delivery.

Technically, testing is about finding defects, but it's also about making sure the requirements are met.

Getting clearly articulated requirements can be difficult. We need the users' perspective, and the users are often too busy to define precisely what they need.

Remember that picture from Chapter 1 where the user wants a car but gets a bicycle? The too-busy user created more work for the company and had to expend more effort himself. After getting the bicycle, he had to explain the problem he was trying to solve in more detail and then wait longer for a better solution.

> The time not taken to define what's needed at the beginning is not saved – rather, more time is spent having to refine an incomplete requirement in order to get a satisfactory solution.

Various techniques exist for getting complete requirements early, but one thing is sure: telling busy users it's in their best interest— even though it is — is rarely a successful strategy. Asking, telling, or demanding may work, but usually it's not effective.

Because good test design depends on having clear requirements, we need a successful strategy to get them in place.

> The best route to obtaining clear requirements leverages the organization's culture and politics.

Some organizations solve the "busy user" problem by creating a role — often called a business analyst — that represents the users' application needs. When the test results come in, you ask the user or business analyst if the outcome was successful: "Is this what you wanted?"

The user already has a picture in mind about what success looks like. What if we ask at the start how the user will recognize success? The answers — successful-outcome statements — are a very good way to expand the requirements.

While this is a valuable technique, it doesn't help when requirements are missing, so how can we assure completeness?

Perhaps the best way to come up with complete requirements is through formal verification. Software engineers have used this process for many years. It was developed by Michael Fagan in the 1970s and many documents are available to describe the process. (See, for example, *Software Formal Inspections Guidebook*, published by NASA as NASA-GB-A302.)

We describe another solution, behavioral modeling, in Chapter 3. We've found users are more willing to review behavioral models than text, and their review is a powerful way to ensure that they understand the requirements and that the requirements are complete.

So far we've used the term "requirements" very generally, but there are many types of requirements:

- End-user requirements
- Operational requirements
- Platform requirements
- Corporate requirements
- Compliance requirements
- Software requirements, or functional requirements

We won't go into these in depth, other than to say that they all need to be considered. Unfortunately, most people only consider end-user requirements in their project planning.

Software requirements (last on the list) are often called specifications. There's an important distinction between end-user requirements and specifications:

> End-user requirements address the problem to be solved.
>
> Specifications describe a solution to the problem.

If the contractor had prepared a specification in our car-vs.-bicycle example and presented it to the user, the problem would have been cleared up well before the bicycle was built, umbrella and all.

Let's focus on exploring the relationship between the requirements and testing. (Plenty of texts discuss best practices for requirements gathering; for example, *Mastering the Requirements Process* by James and Suzanne Robertson.)

Requirements are the means of communication between business and IT. Because of their importance in the MQM, we include Requirements Verification as a test stage.

During the Requirements Verification stage, we take the following steps:

1. Build a common reference for business analysts and IT.
2. Document the separate business functions
3. Link the requirements with the common reference.
4. Add proof points to each requirement.

Build a Common Reference

We start with the end user's perspective. We need to get the end user to articulate the business functions he uses during work hours. This approach is independent of whether we're modifying software that is already in place or we're building a new system from scratch.

First we make a list of the business functions or activities the end user performs. We'll group them to handle them easier.

We break down and separate the functions with representatives of the business side and the requirements engineer. Consider the following guidelines:

A business function supports a basic end-user activity — it's a step in the business process. The business function has a testable result. Thumb rules for breaking down the application into business functions are:

- Each use case, or basic end-user activity, is a business function.
- If a group of use cases is very similar, group them together to form one business function.
- If a use case is very large or very complex, split it into two or more business functions.
- To completely test a single business function, we should need no more than 30 to 40 positive test cases.

Adapt those guidelines and interpret them according to the project environment. Usually projects using object-oriented methodology have a different view on functionality than projects using structured analysis and design.

However, keep in mind that the functionality the business needs in order to support its work is independent from the underlying methodology. We can derive the business functionality using this guideline.

Here's a sample application that keeps customer contact information. In a given application environment, the functional breakdown would look like Table 1.

Customer Contact
Incoming customer contact
Outgoing customer contact
Create customer
Identify customer
Register interaction
Change/maintain customer information
Customer message

Table 1: Sample business functions of a customer contact application

Document the Separate Business Functions

To document the business function breakdown, we build requirements into a tree structure. One way this can be implemented is in the Mercury Quality Center™ (for more information, see Appendix B). The tree structure has the basic elements shown in Figure 9.

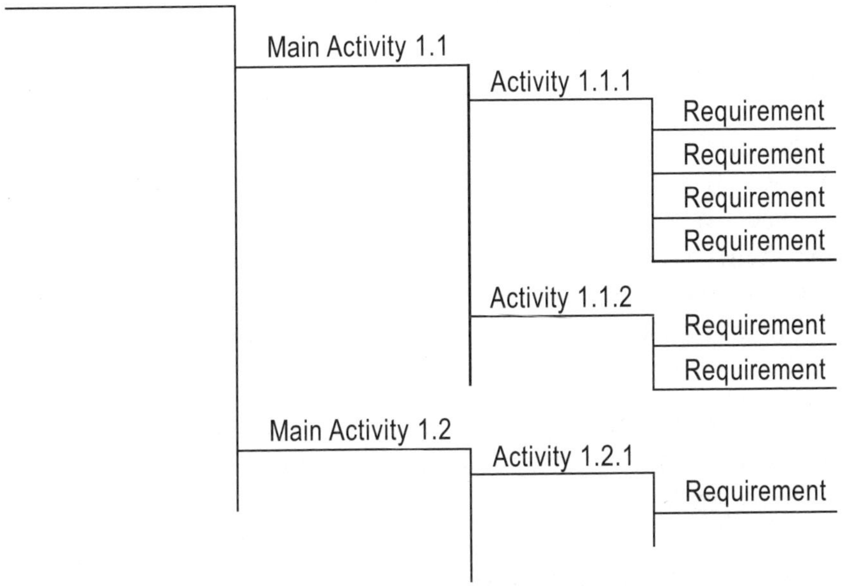

Figure 9: Sample requirements structure

For our customer contact example, the structure would look like Figure 10.

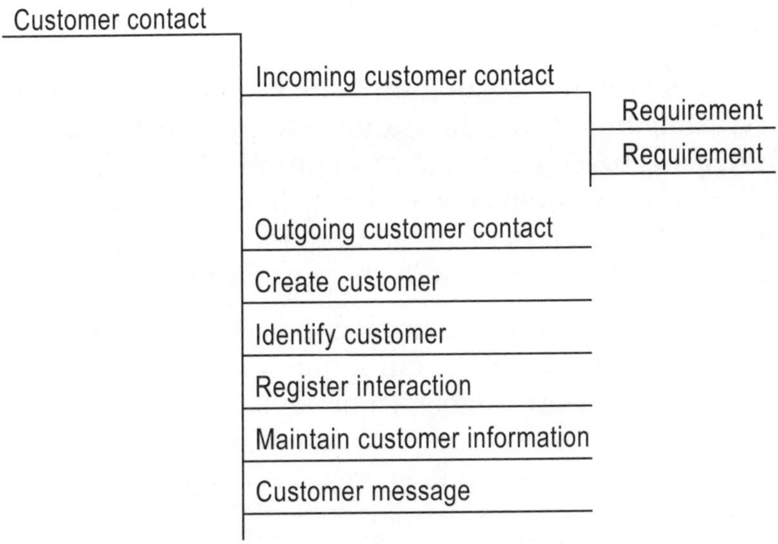

Figure 10: Customer contact requirements structure

Link Requirements into the Structure

Most companies document requirements independently, without structure, in tools like Word, Excel, Lotus Notes, or Outlook. In this step, we link the requirement documents in the Quality Center with the appropriate business functions. This way, we create a direct mapping between the structure of the business activity from the business perspective and the detailed requirements for each of the business functions.

We can use this mapping for reporting and analysis purposes to find out which business areas are covered by requirements and which are not.

Define Proof Points

Most requirements testing approaches use review techniques where people work through the written requirement to find the issues and complete them. These techniques can be very effective at the beginning of a project to create a new software application.

However, modifying existing software is much more common than creating brand-new applications from scratch. For requirements based on changes, we introduce "proof points." These are simple statements of exactly how one would recognize that a requirement has been met. (Proof points can, of course, be used for new software applications as well.)

Think about what would make an end user sign off on this requirement. For example, if our requirement is to build a house, we ask ourselves what list of items would allow us to sign off that the house is complete. Do we want a four-sided brick house? Do we need a kitchen with stainless steel appliances?

> When you think of the questions that would allow you to accept and sign off on the requirement, it will help you create more relevant proof points.

For every requirement, a specific measure of compliance needs to be in place, and you must be able to demonstrate that the requirement has been met. That is, you must be able to perform a test concerning that requirement.

The process is this: Each requirement must have within it a statement of the acceptance criteria. We then translate the product requirement and acceptance criteria into a test requirement, which tells precisely how to determine if the requirement has been met.

Using our customer contact example, let's extend the requirements tree a bit.

Customer Contact

- Incoming contact
    - Requirement 1: display customer ID from incoming telephone number.
    - Requirement 2: system automatically answers the call within four rings.

Stated this way, two things emerge. First, it is relatively easy to create proof points based on questions:

- What would satisfy the requirement here?
- Are we okay with any customer ID displayed?
- Do we need the customer ID to be the telephone number?
- Can we display something other than the ID?
- Will we accept the system answering calls with more than four rings?

- What about no rings?
- Are we okay if the system does not automatically answer the phone?

By asking these questions, we come up with the following proof points:

- Correct customer ID is based on the telephone number.
- Only a customer ID is displayed.
- The call has to be answered automatically.
- The call has to be answered within four rings.

Then another question emerges: What if the call comes from an unrecognized number? This question can lead us to additional requirements and show us that we need additional tests.

Requirements are usually hierarchical in nature, going from the general to the specific. We can lay these out in a tree structure as shown in Figure 10, with all related requirements gathered together in each branch of the tree. The requirements structure guides the test-plan creation and the test-plan tree matches the requirements tree.

> The execution plan for any test uses the test-requirements tree overlaid with the priority of each of the requirements, so the testing focuses on the most important items first.

We determine the priority using the business risk calculations, which we will discuss in detail in Chapter 5, along with technical IT considerations. Although some elements may not be high priority from a business perspective, they may be vital for the proper execution of the business functions. For example, most business people are not so much interested in network protocols, but without success in this area, the business processes could fail.

Because we base the test plan on the requirements, it becomes a simple matter to understand the status of any requirement during the course of the test. It's possible to look for a specific requirement, for example, to be a certain percentage complete.

We can also report on the percentage of requirements the test cases have covered. Determining the business risks associated with testing is possible by analyzing how well we've covered the requirements.

One way of implementing this is to start with a 100 percent risk of failure at the beginning of the development life cycle. As tests cover the requirements and are passed, we lower the risk, until ideally the risk becomes zero before we make the go-live decision.

> We present the test status in terms that make sense to the business users and the tests are aligned with business outcomes.

A slightly more sophisticated approach takes the priorities of the requirements into account. By prioritizing the requirements, and aligning the testing with those priorities, we can assure that the important things are done first. That way, if, as often happens, we run out of time, we can be sure that we have reduced risk as much as possible.

Status reports then can discuss the coverage percent for High, Medium, and Low priority requirements. Of course, if the reports indicate that 100 percent of the Low priority requirements have been tested and 0 percent of the High priority requirements have been tested, we'd have to revisit the planning activity!

Now that we understand what to test and how to align what to test with the business outcomes, the next step is to design the actual tests. Many organizations do this in an ad-hoc fashion. In the next chapter, we show you a more effective test design method.

Chapter 3

Behavioral Modeling: A Practical Way to Design Efficient, Effective Tests

The test design process in most organizations amounts to "smart folks dream up cool things to do." Our approach to the testing process is to find out how the thing you are testing (or in more technical terms, the article under test) will behave in various circumstances. We do this by modeling the behavior of the AUT and get a result that makes product development more efficient.

One of the main tenets of behavioral modeling is that it starts with breaking down the product or process you want to test into independent functions. What pieces can we look at that operate independently of other bits? We can then design tests for those pieces. We call this process *functional decomposition*.

We use graphics to describe the behavior of independent functions. We call this *behavioral modeling*. It's a simple process really — we ask only two questions when we are breaking down (or decomposing) a piece of software into independent functions:

1. What does it do? In other words, what is the actual behavior of the function — what is it doing? It is an active, not a passive function we are trying to get at.
2. What influences the behavior? By learning what influences the behavior, you can find the control points you'll use in testing.

How do we go about making this model? We do this graphically. (See Figure 11 through Figure 14.)

To look at the functionality of the AUT, we make a graphical description of its functional behavior. At a very high level, we begin by laying out the end user's process.

This sounds easy, but when you try it, it may seem incredibly difficult — until you get some practice at it. Don't be discouraged. The key is practice, practice, practice. When we teach workshops, we spend a lot of time just having people create drawings. In some ways, creating these graphics is a bit like riding a bicycle. You can't really learn how to ride a bicycle by reading a book. You have to get out there and start pedaling.

Bigger

We're going to start with a very simple example of behavioral modeling. Let's look at a little function we'll call *bigger.*

The function takes two numeric values as input. It returns a value of "+1" if the first of the two inputs is *bigger* than the second — hence the name of the function. It returns a value of "-1" if the first number is smaller than the second and, finally, it returns a value of "0" if the numbers are equal.

That's it. That is the entire, complete specification of *bigger.* To model the behavior of *bigger,* we make a visual picture of it (Figure 11):

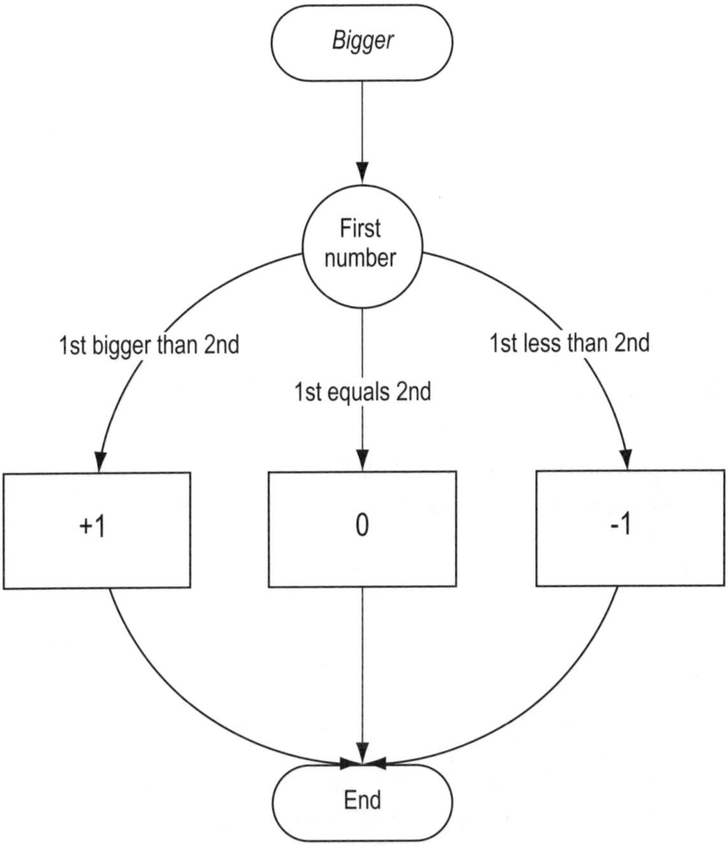

Figure 11: Bigger behavioral model (a)

First, let's examine the shape of the blocks used in this model. The oval marks the beginning or end of the model.

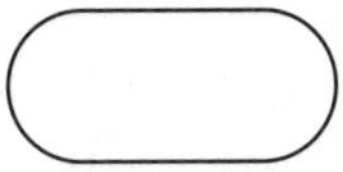

Figure 12: Oval represents the terminator

Next, is the circle, which represents case logic. The circle indicates that any of several possibilities may be chosen.

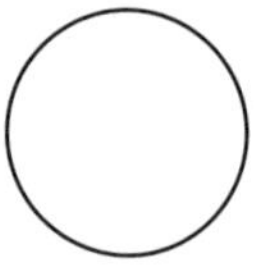

Figure 13: Circle represents case logic

Third is the rectangle, which shows the result we expect when we execute a test along a path. It's not strictly necessary to include the result in the behavior model. We've included it here for clarification; but in some situations, putting the result symbol in the model makes it more complex, and so harder to use. If it doesn't help model the behavior, don't use it.

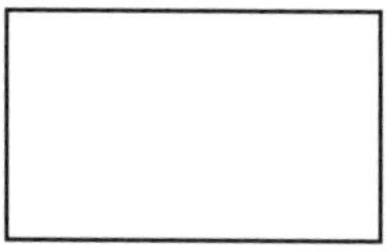

Figure 14: Rectangle represents the result

As we look at *bigger,* we clearly see three branches, each of which represents a separate test case. This graphic shows us each test case and the results we expect from that test case.

If we ask our basic behavior modeling questions, we want to know first what it does. The AUT here is a piece of software that reads two numbers, compares them, and reports the relationship between them.

Next, we need to know what influences the behavior. The relative values of the numbers influence the behavior.

Notice that something subtle is happening here. In Figure 11, that first circle implies that there are two numbers. What if there are more than two numbers? Fewer than two? What if they aren't numbers? Our specification for *bigger* did not address these important points. When we lay things out graphically, the model helps us to identify things that are missing, unsaid, or assumed. Let's redraw the model in Figure 15 considering a few more points.

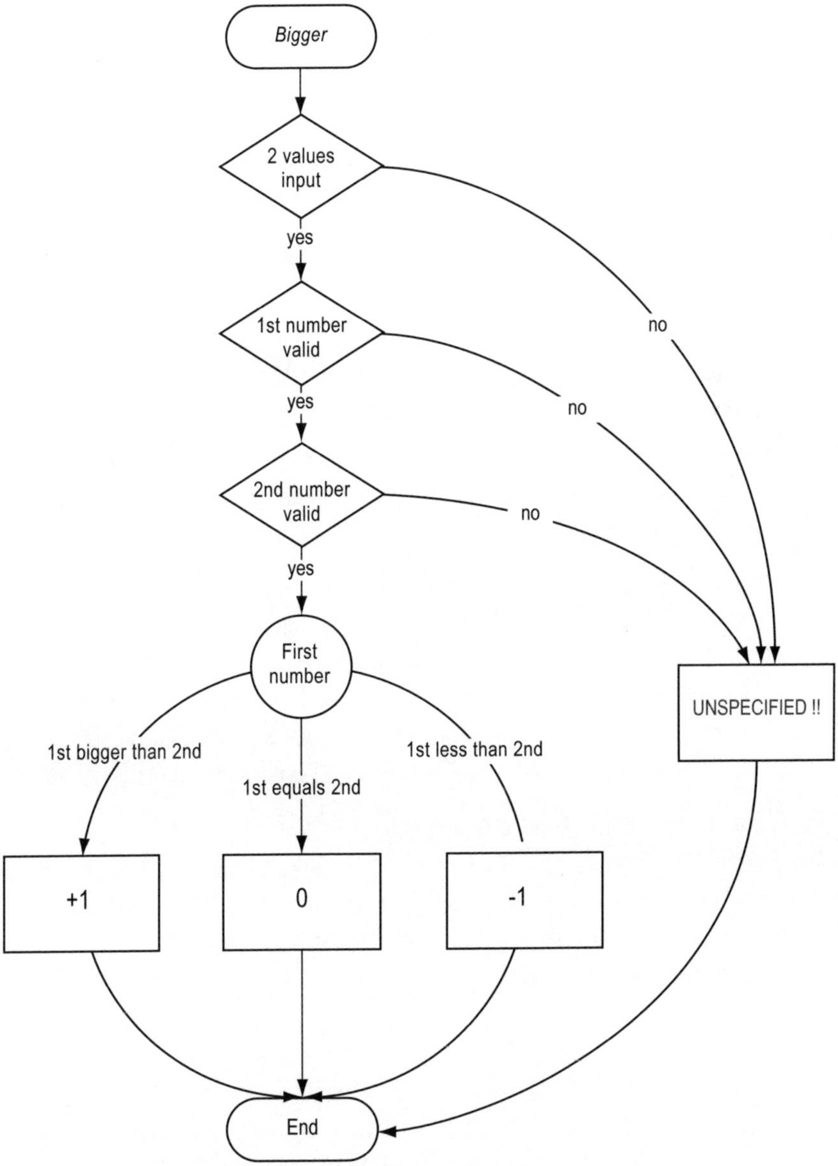

Figure 15: Bigger behavioral model (b)

We have introduced a new shape in the model: the diamond, which indicates a decision.

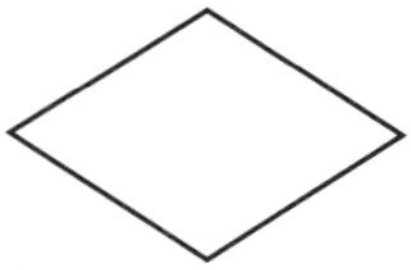

Figure 16: Diamond represents a decision

The decision diamond represents a binary choice: yes or no; true or false. If you're familiar with flowcharts, you'll recognize this symbol.

But we need to distinguish between a flowchart and a behavioral model:

- In a flowchart, you describe the logic of the program. At a decision point in a flow chart, the program asks a question and reacts to the answer.
- In a behavioral model, there is no question. A tester makes decisions rather than asks questions, so the decision diamond represents the choice the test designer makes. We don't ask if there are, for example, two input values. We'll set up tests so on one path there will be two values and on the other there will not be.

When we look at Figure 15, we can see the reason for predicting the results of any one particular test. Notice those three paths that go to the box labeled "unspecified." We have identified defects in the specification merely by attempting to diagram the functionality.

> If 70 percent of the defects in software are introduced at the requirements or specification phase, we can see that diagramming the function helps us to spot those defects and improve the product.

So, we've identified a hole in the specification. When developers are faced with a hole in the specification, what do they do? That depends on the developer's level of experience. An experienced senior developer will go back to whoever produced the specification and ask what is supposed to happen and see that the specification is updated with this information. The intermediate developer will try to figure out what's supposed to happen and code to that. The rookie does nothing — rookies don't even notice the hole in the specification.

The same thing is true of testers — they respond differently, depending on their experience. Our tests must conclude whether the program works as specified.

But first, we must be sure the specification is complete, clear, and correct. Notice that in Figure 15 we left the results as "unspecified." To figure out what's going on, go back to the author of the specification, get clarification, and make sure the author updates the specification with the clarification. That's the only way to be sure that the entire team has the same understanding.

> Testers should never make up specifications. If you find yourself doing this, stop it! Stop it right now!

Our task is to find the defects, remember? The real problem is that if the tester makes up a specification, the developer may also be making up a specification. The specification the tester makes up and the specification the developer makes up may differ, and we wind up with a mismatch between the testing and the developing.

The best way to reduce the number of problems in requirement and specification documents is to conduct formal reviews or verifications. We do not address verification in detail in this book. However, you'll find an overview of the verification process in Appendix F.

Back to *bigger*. We have more things to consider. For example, we could think about the type of data we have: numbers. Are they decimal? Are they scientific notation?

While it may be hard to see with something as simple as *bigger*, keep in mind that a one-to-one correspondence between paths in the behavioral model and number of test cases does not necessarily exist. It's close, but in some situations, there may be more or fewer test cases than paths.

As an example, suppose *bigger* could execute on any of three different platforms: Windows, Mac, and UNIX. If this were the case, the behavioral model would need to account for this. The resulting model would look like Figure 17.

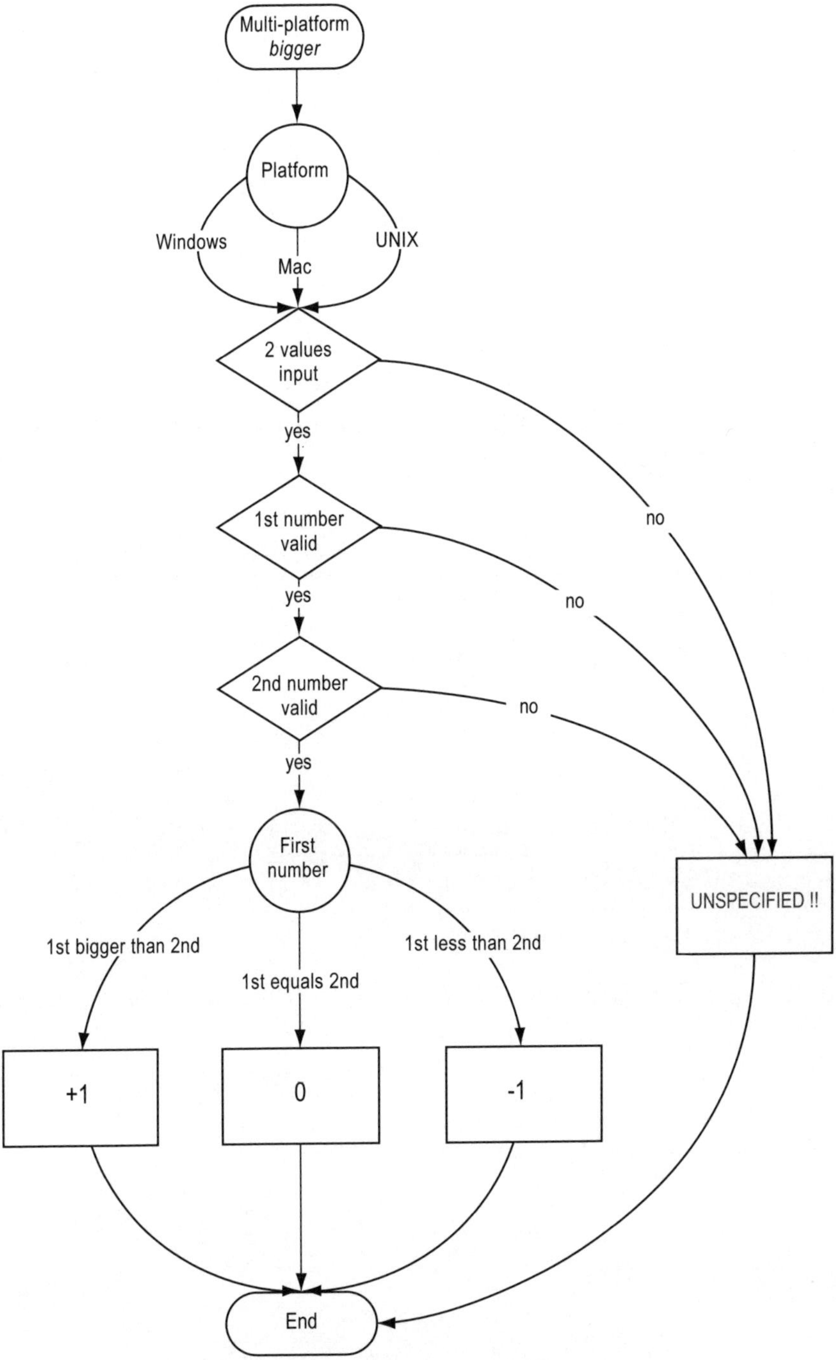

Figure 17: Bigger behavioral model (c)

If you count the number of paths through the model, you find a total of 18 paths — the six we started with, multiplied by the number of platforms. If the architecture is such that the same executable code is used in each of the platforms, then you could plan the test cases so some of them are executed in one platform, others in another platform, and the remainder in the final platform, thus dropping from 18 test cases back to six. The decision is, as usual, a risk decision.

Finally, let's clean up the "unspecified" result. We will have gone back to the author of the specification, reported this problem, and he or she updated the specs. We now know that there are return codes given for different possible outcomes as listed in Table 2.

Condition	**Return code**
First number bigger than the second	+1
First number equal to the second	0
First number smaller than the second	-1
Not two input values	-97
First input value non-numeric	-98
Second input value non-numeric	-99

Table 2: Return codes for outcomes

Finally, we have the real, complete behavior model for *bigger* in Figure 18.

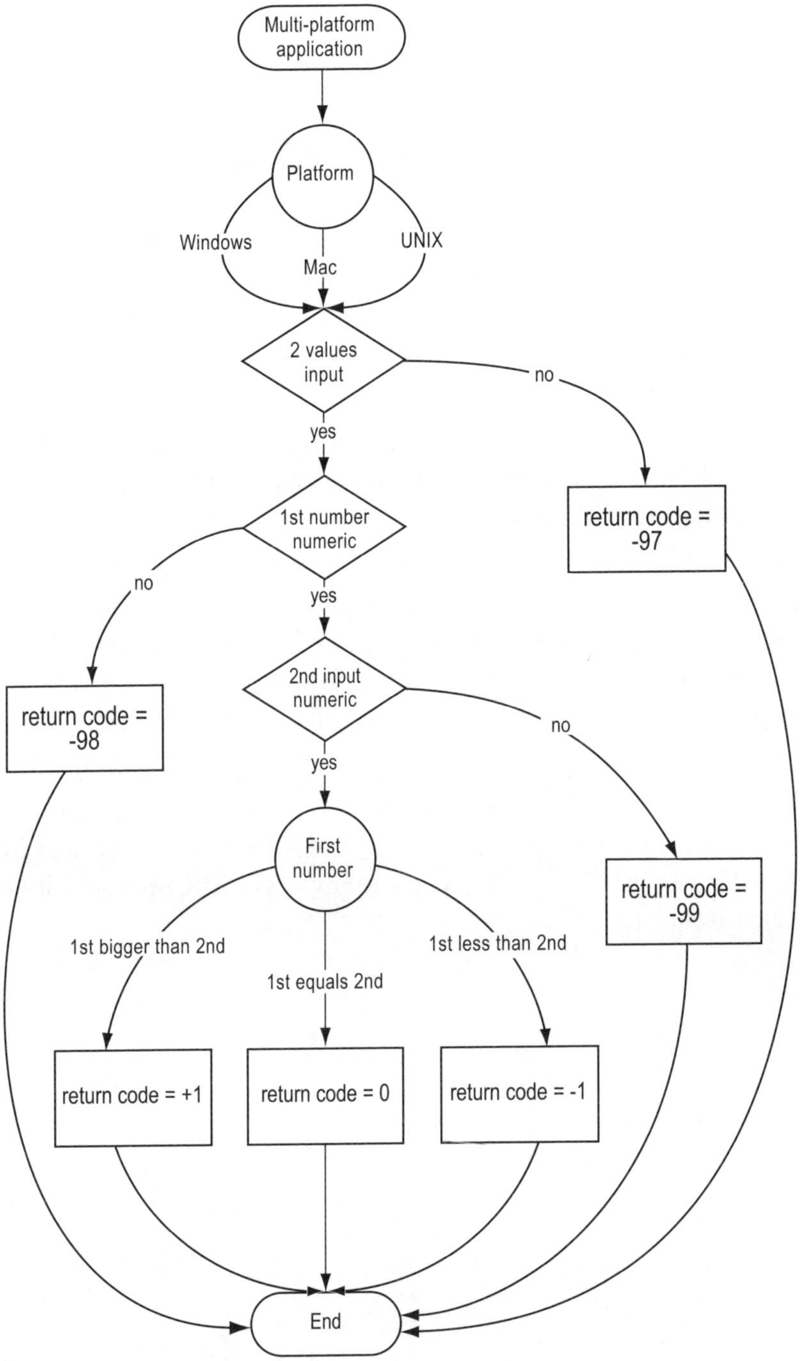

Figure 18: Final bigger behavioral model

Remember, this is *not* a flowchart. It is a behavioral model. An example demonstrates the distinction quite clearly a bit later on, when we look at our *triangle* example.

FAST: Testing a Simple ATM

If we look at something a bit more complex than *bigger*, we can introduce a few more concepts. Let's consider a banking application — the familiar automated teller machine (ATM). Our ATM is a very simple one so that we can use it to demonstrate how to do test design.

We call our ATM the "functionally advanced sidewalk teller" (FAST). It can deposit to or withdraw from a checking account or a savings account, transfer money between those two accounts, and tell you your balance in either of the accounts.

Even though it's a pretty simple application, to try and diagram all of it on one page would be difficult. We're going to divide it into subsections. We call this process *functional decomposition*. We're dividing the AUT into independent areas.

By independent, we mean operationally independent. We look for parts of the application that can be tested independently from the other parts. (Of course, there's always interaction in a computing product, but we look for ways to minimize this in our test design.)

Let's try a first pass at the functional decomposition of *FAST*. What does it do? See Figure 19.

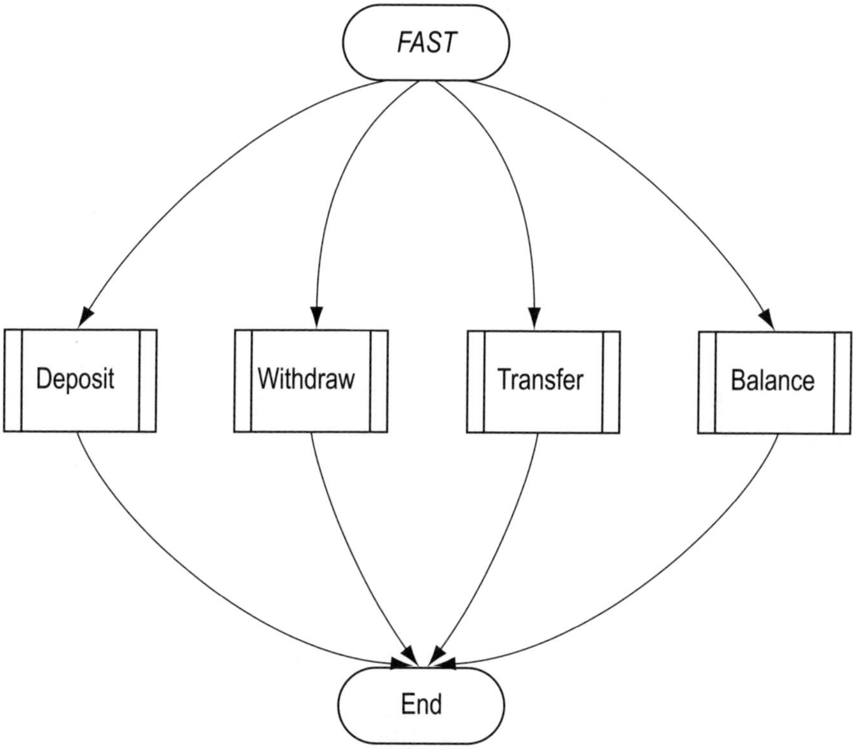

Figure 19: FAST behavioral model (a)

We have just introduced another shape: the striped rectangle or defined process.

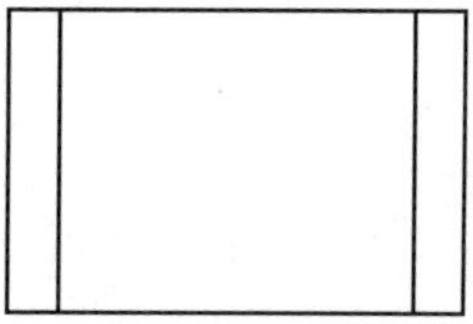

Figure 20: Striped rectangle represents a defined process

A *defined process* means that the process is defined in a lower-level diagram — we are drilling down into more discrete parts.

In the ATM example, testers can put themselves in the place of the user, supplying their own external knowledge of the process. When you walk up to a teller machine, the first thing you do is put in your card — that little piece of plastic the bank gave you — and type in your password or personal identification number (PIN).

We need to include a defined process examining the sign-on functionality. So let's add this to our diagram for the test suite in Figure 21.

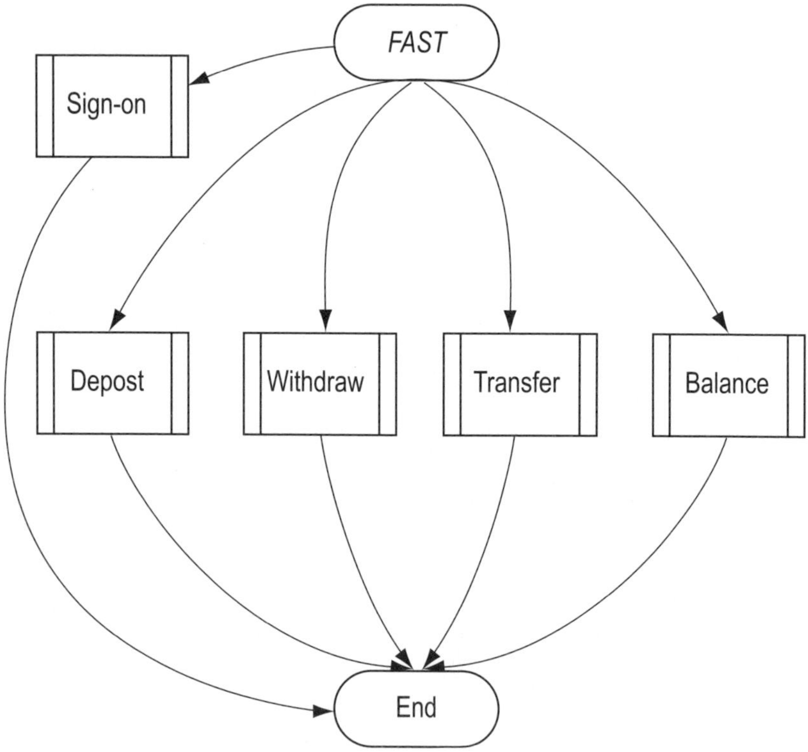

Figure 21: FAST behavioral model (b)

We know we have to sign on in order to do anything, so why do we need a separate defined process for sign-on?

Let's do some arithmetic. Assume for the moment that there are 10 different paths through the sign-on functionality and 10 different paths through *deposit*. If we were to test them both together, that would mean 100 different ways to get through the combination of *sign-on* and *deposit,* or 100 test cases. If we test them separately, there are only 20 test cases. We always look for ways to add the number of test cases, not multiply the numbers.

This suggests some very important principles of functional decomposition.

> Using something isn't testing it.

We *use* sign-on to get to the other functions, but we only *test* sign-on in its own set of test cases.

> Assume what's not being directly tested is perfect.

This is a difficult assumption, but it's important to simplify our test suite. Assume that *sign-on* works and get on with the business of testing *deposit*. To put it another way, in testing *deposit,* we don't really care if all of the ins and outs of *sign-on* are correct, as long as we can find some that allow us to move ahead.

The various actions one can take have a certain amount of commonality among them. If we look at some of the error cases, or exceptional cases, we can say that, in general, it doesn't matter whether you're trying to deposit, withdraw, transfer, or see a balance. For example, suppose the printer runs out of paper. Let's create a separate process for these exception cases in Figure 22.

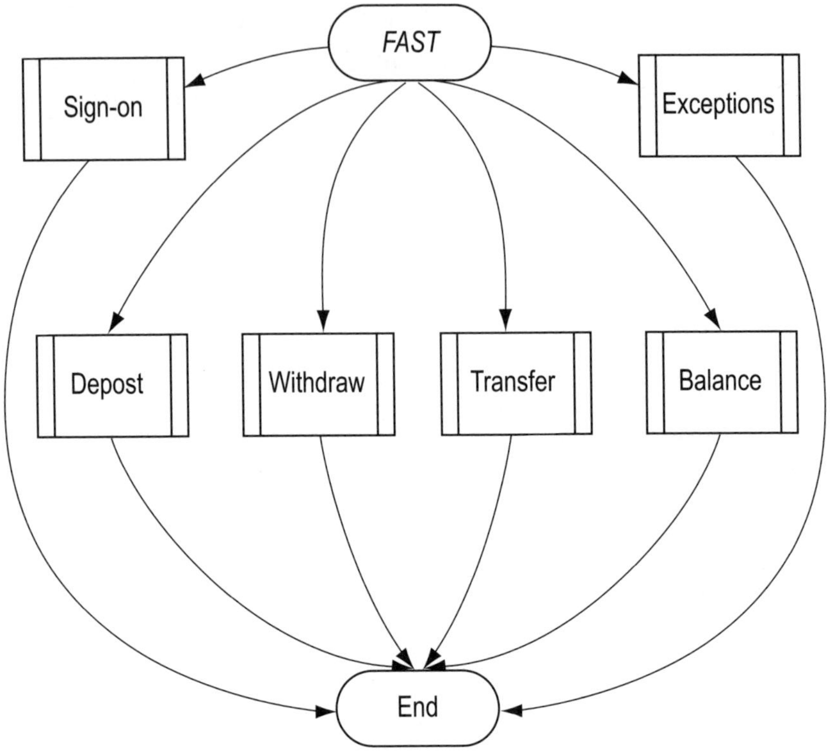

Figure 22: FAST behavioral model (c)

Sometimes, despite our best efforts of breaking down the AUT into independent functions, we're still left with the possibility of interactions between them. For example, we might wonder if the system under test is left in a precarious state after the execution of a function. Just to be on the safe side, we'll create one more defined process, one that considers combinations of functions or *strings*.

Figure 23 shows us the complete behavioral model of *FAST* at a high level.

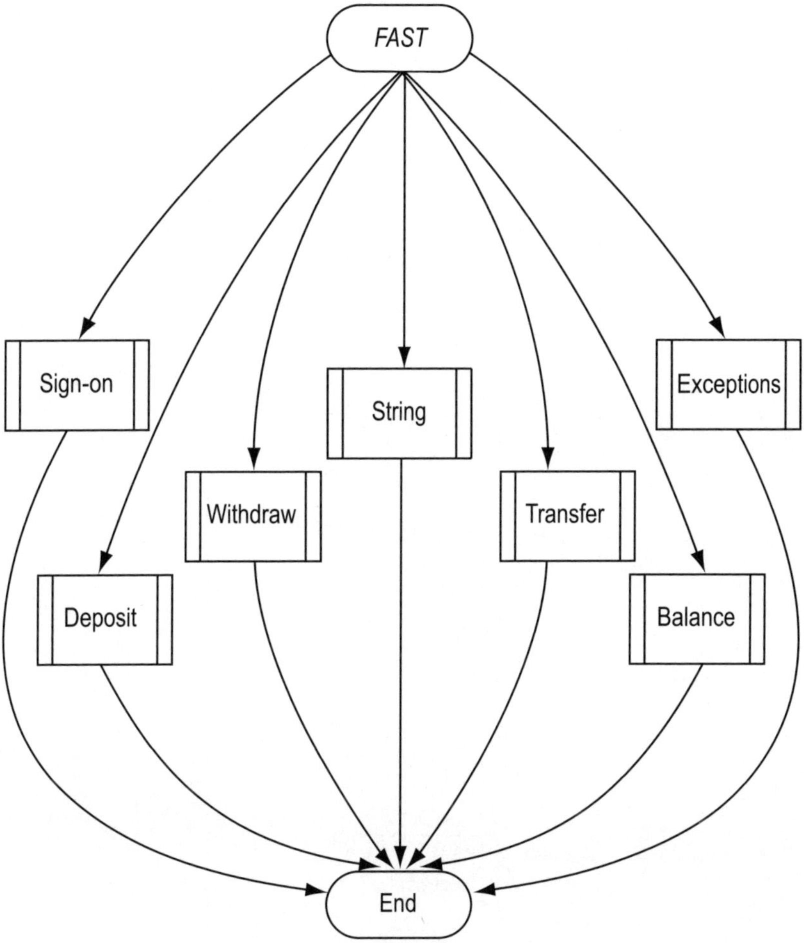

Figure 23: FAST behavioral model (d)

Let's redraw it one more time, a bit more neatly, in Figure 24.

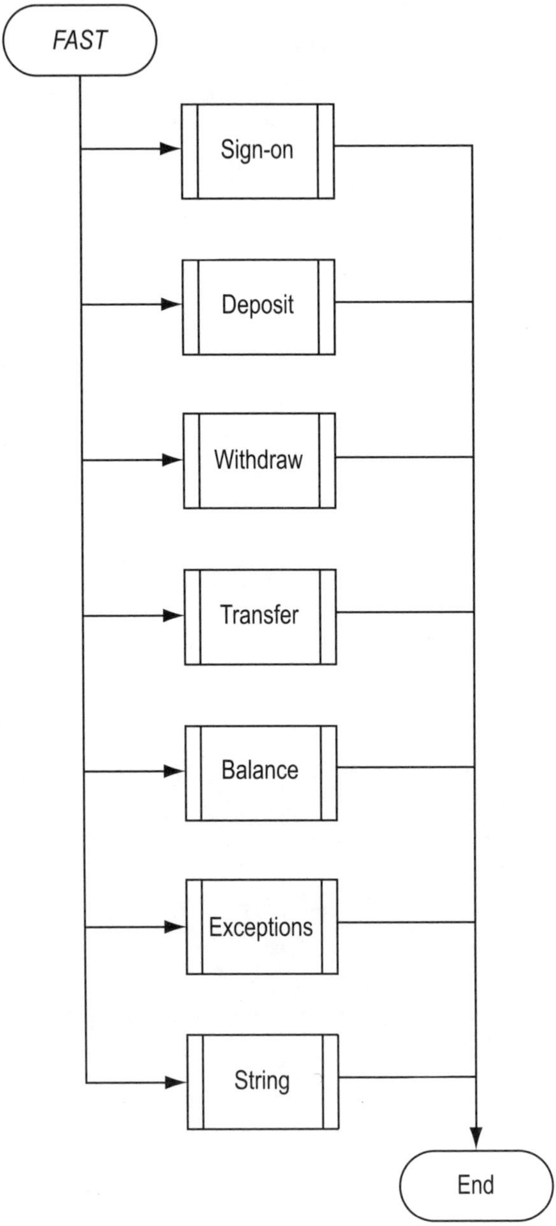

Figure 24: FAST behavioral model (e)

We'll dive a little deeper here, and show you some of the test designs for a couple of the lower-level processes. And then we'll see how this all hangs together.

Let's turn our attention to the predefined process, *deposit,* in Figure 25.

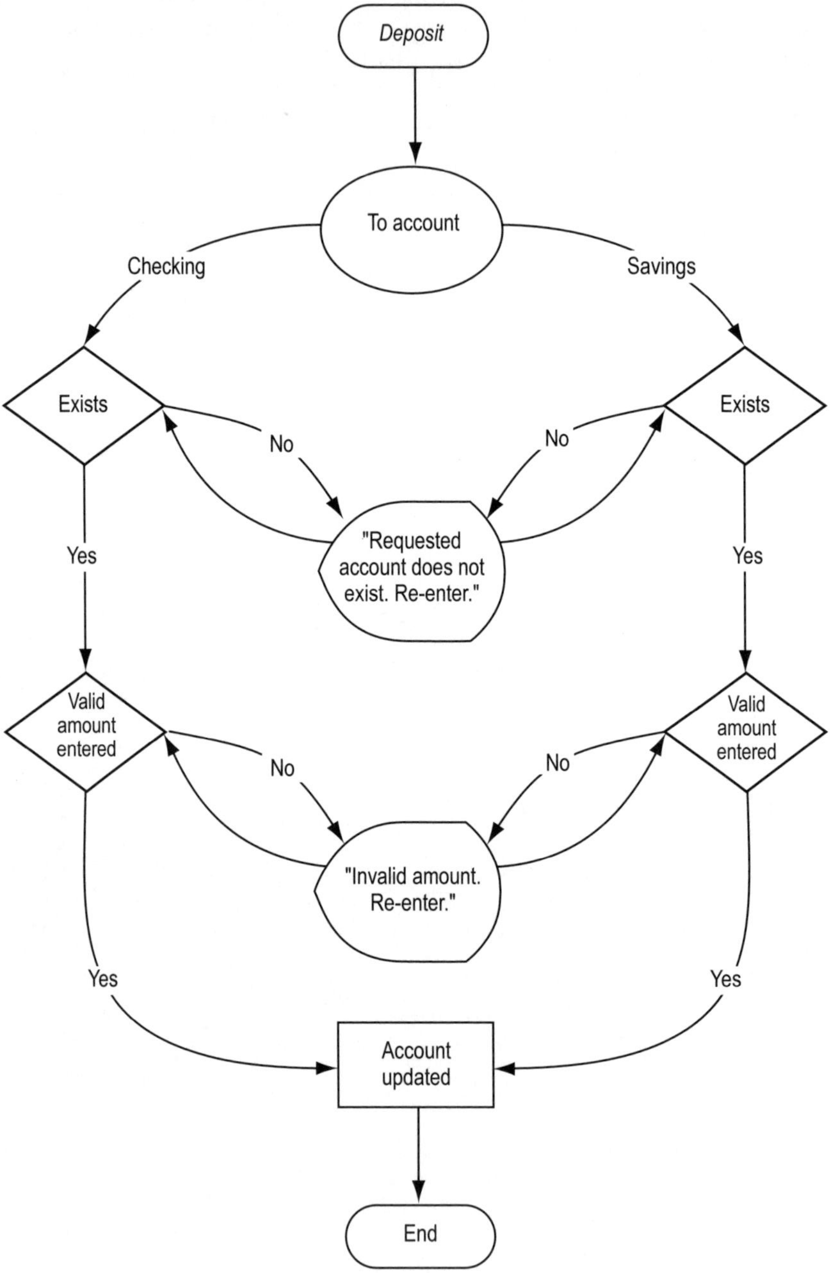

Figure 25: Deposit behavioral model (a)

Two lines come out of the decision block (the diamond). Each line is one of the yes/no choices. For example, one of the decision blocks allows the choice of whether or not the account exists. The choice will be either "yes" or "no."

We also see the display symbol, which indicates information that is displayed on the screen. This symbol tells the tester what to look for during the test. Within the symbol, we indicate the content we expect on the screen. In the examples above, these are the error messages we expect.

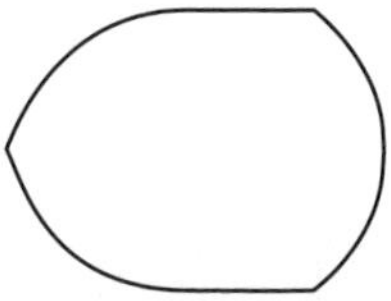

Figure 26: Display symbol

Also notice the lines going into and out of those display symbols. These indicate that in the error condition, an error message is displayed and processing continues. Not all programs behave this way. It's actually more common for a decision point to come after an error, asking the user whether to continue or not.

The display symbol is actually a special case of result. While you may decide not to include result on some paths of your model, it is very rare not to include display.

Let's set the syntax aside and review Figure 25 for content.

If we're on a path in the model where the selected account does not exist, the line indicates that we go back and check again to see if the account exists. What should happen, however, is that we go back earlier in the model to selecting the account. Also, notice that both sides of this diagram are the same — it is symmetrical, which suggests that we can reduce the diagram to something simpler. Take a look at Figure 27.

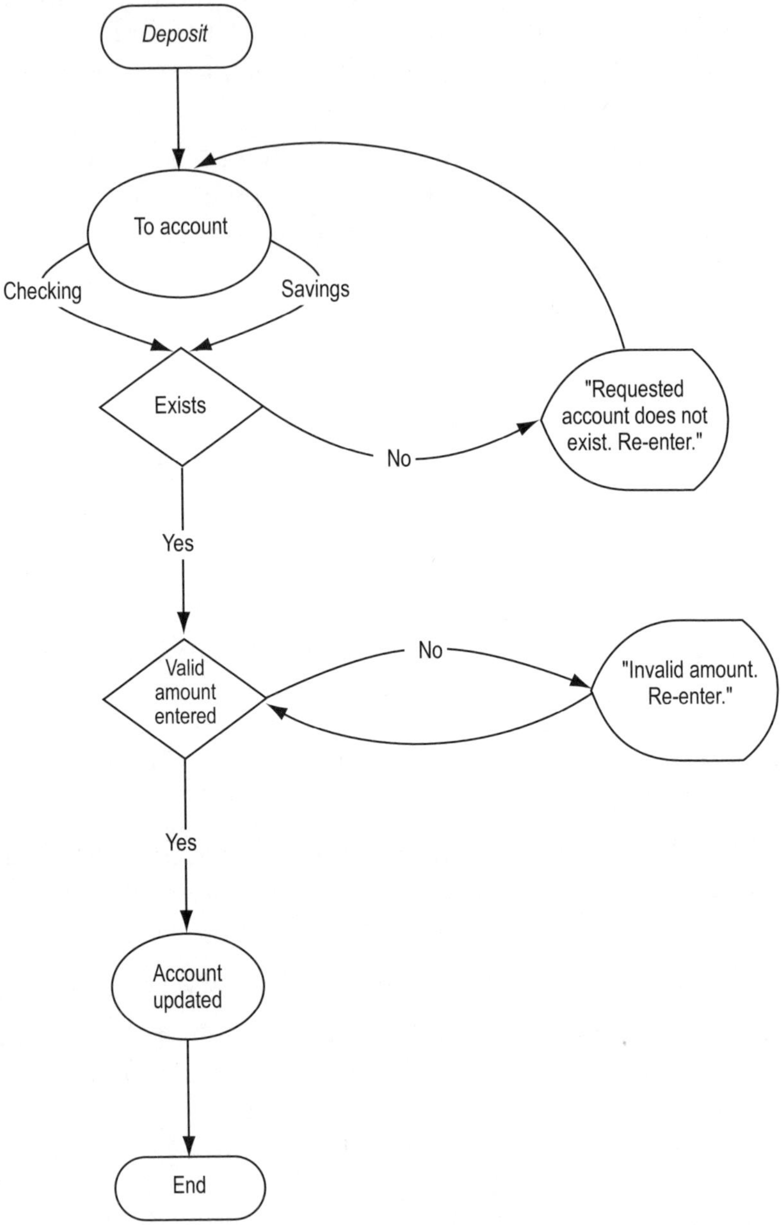

Figure 27: Deposit behavioral model (b)

Other ways of modeling the deposit function may be possible — in testing, it's very rare to have only one right answer — but let's continue to work with this one. The same thing applies when you design your tests.

> Come up with a good design: one that works. Don't spend days, weeks, and months agonizing over the one perfect, best, only true answer. There is none! Get one that works and move forward.

In the next few diagrams, we highlight the paths for some deposit function test cases.

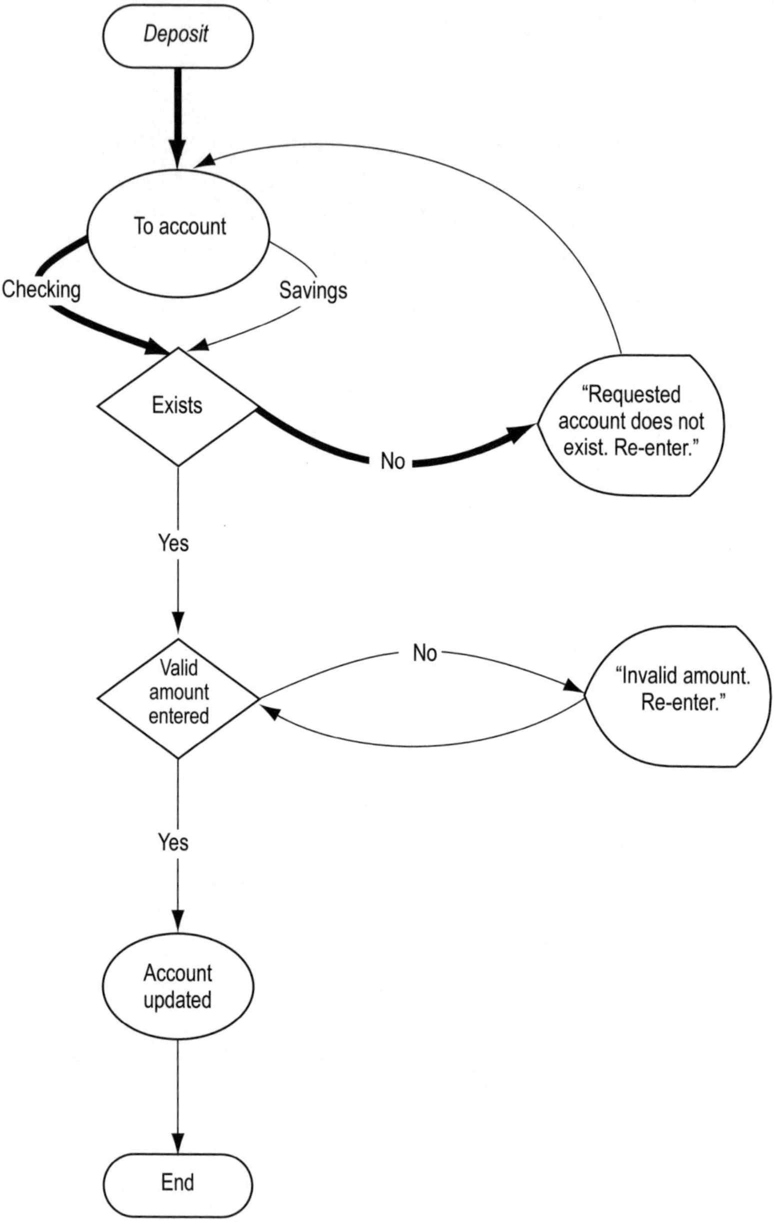

Figure 28: Test path (a)

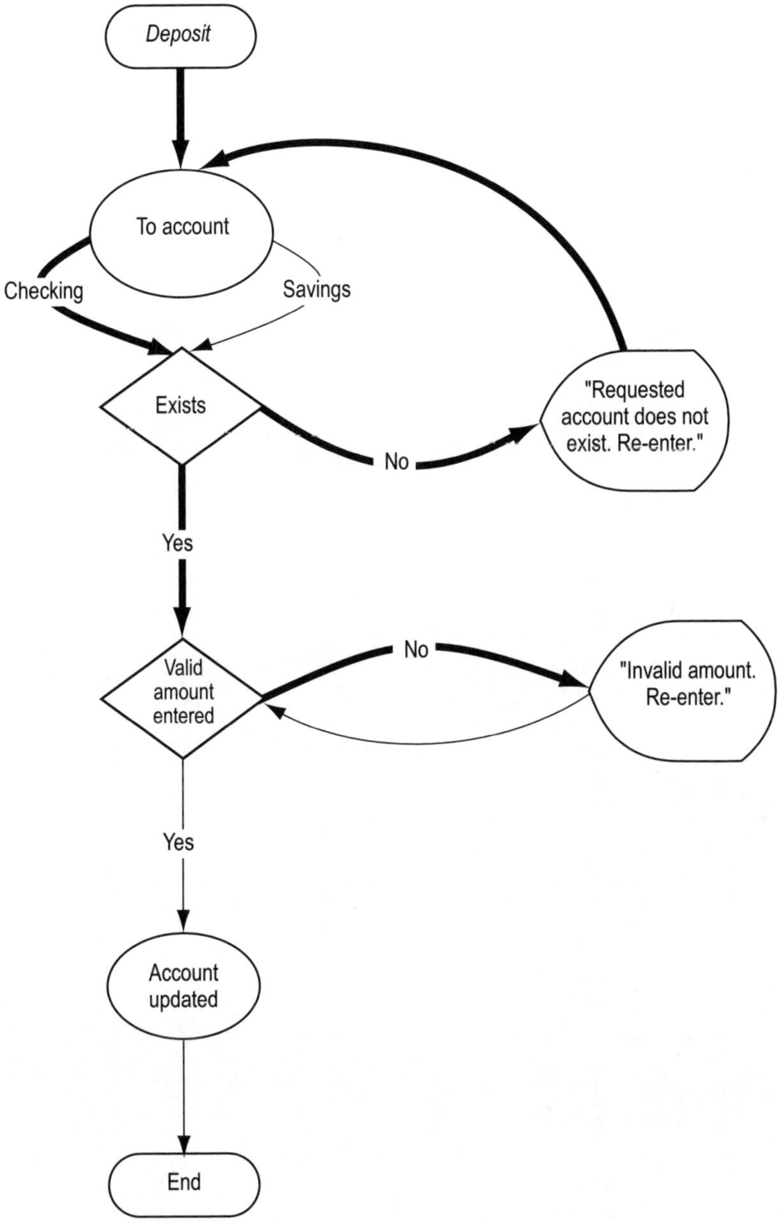

Figure 29: Test path (b)

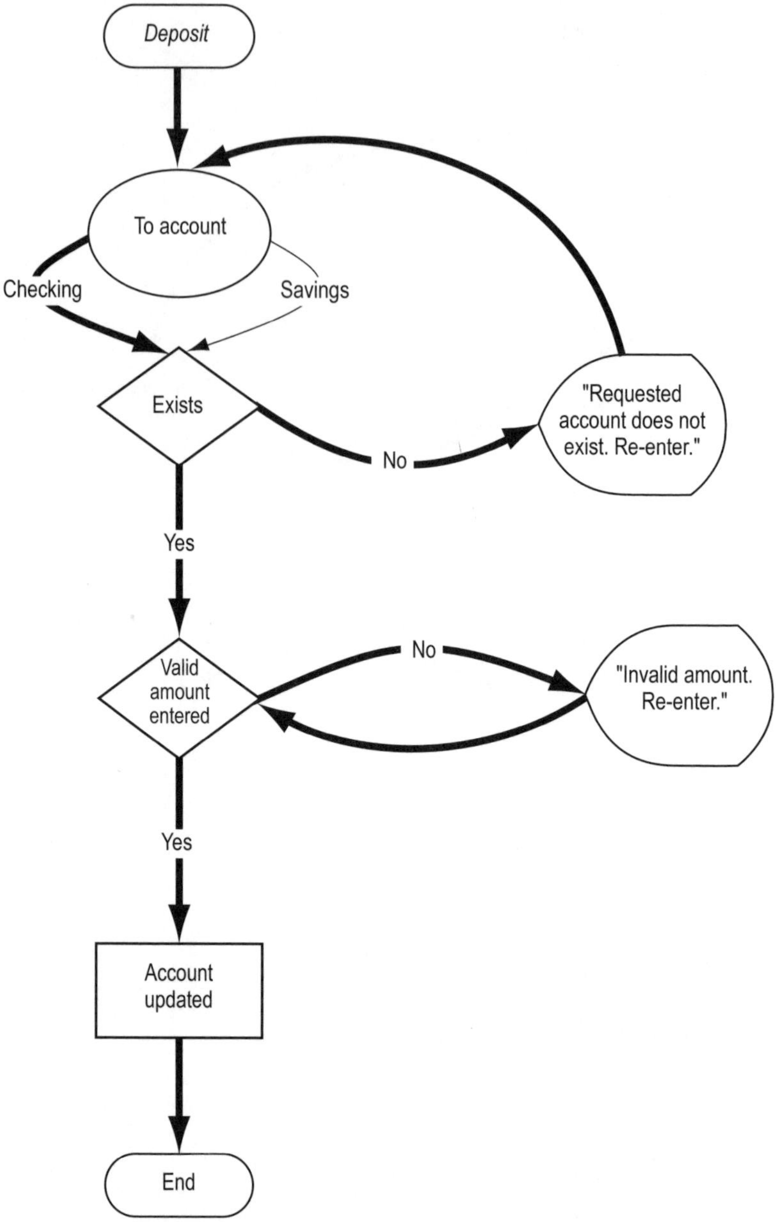

Figure 30: Test path (c)

You should be able to extend the notion of these test paths yourself by now. It's fairly straightforward.

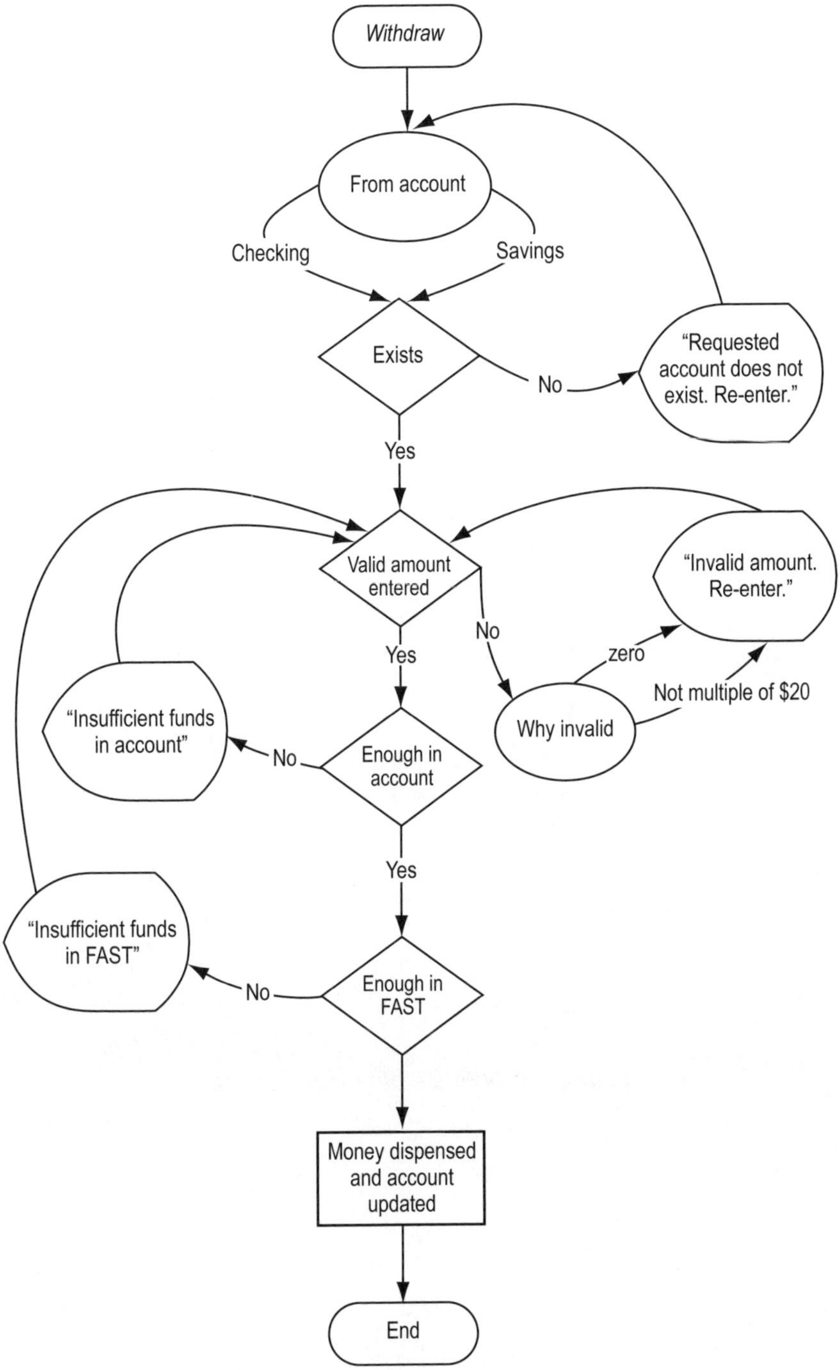

Figure 31: Withdraw behavioral model

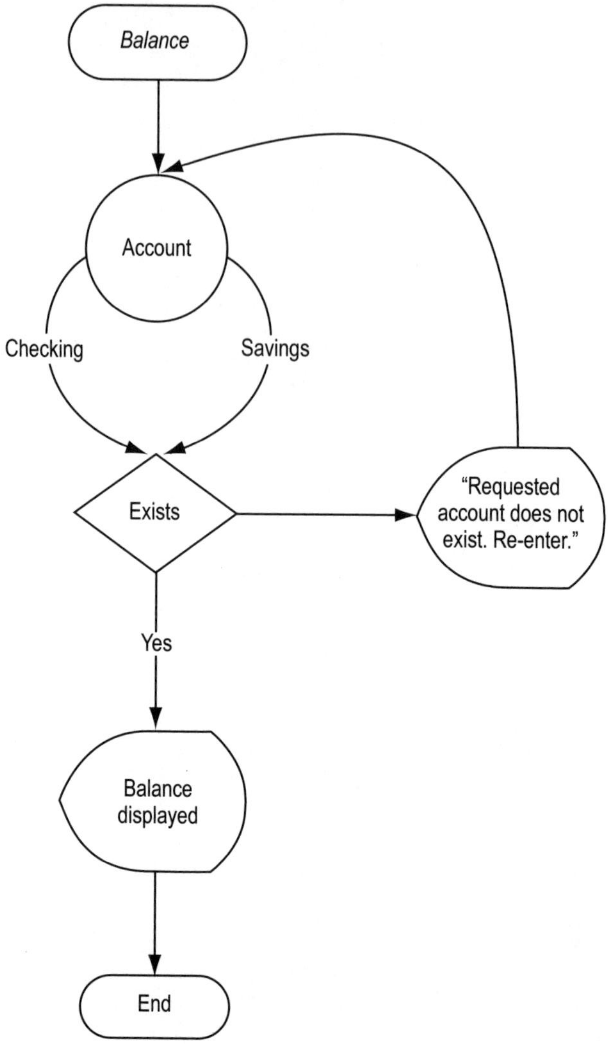

Figure 32: Balance behavioral model

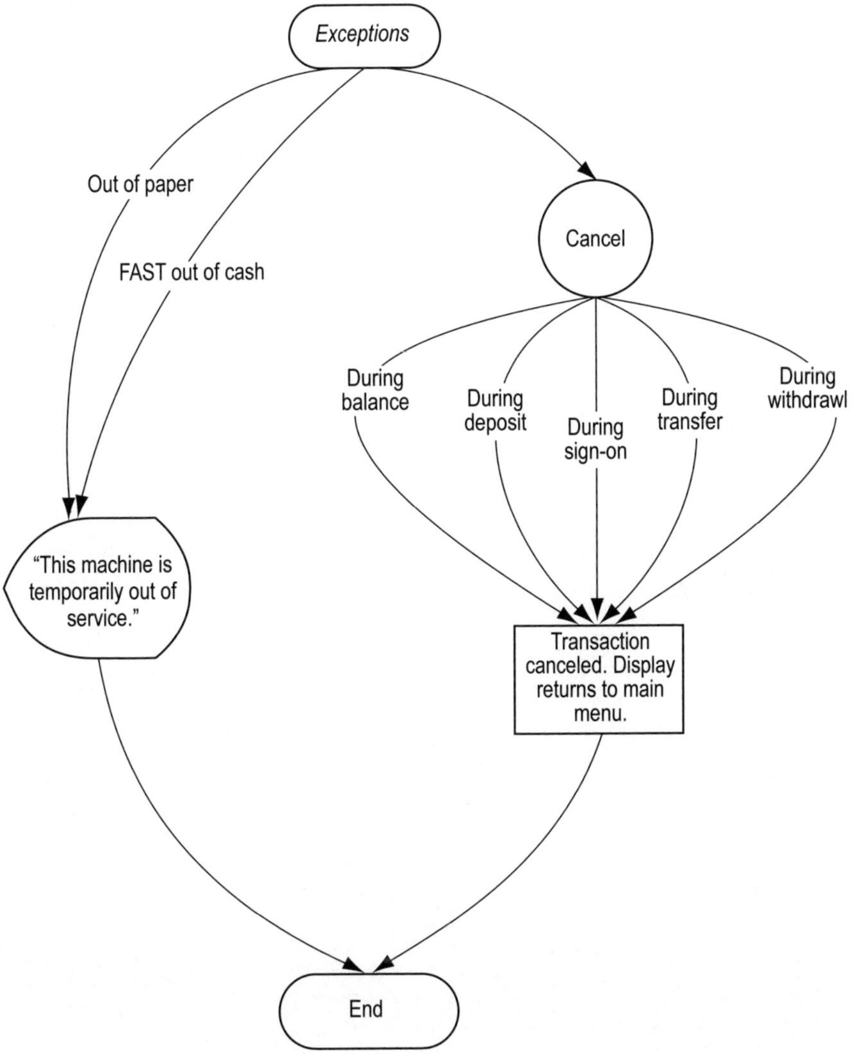

Figure 33: Exceptions behavioral model

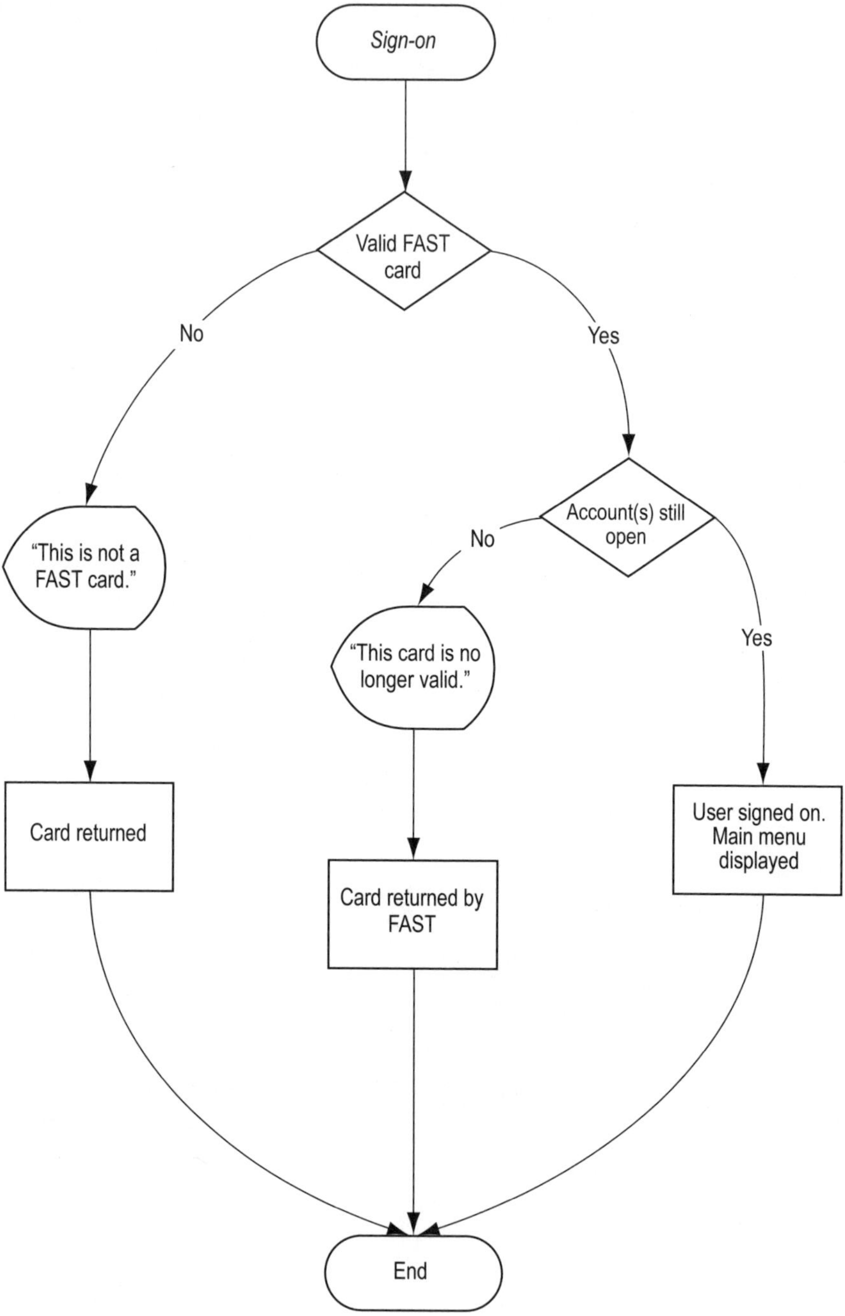

Figure 34: Sign-on behavioral model

The last function from our high-level behavior model is *string*, which addresses the interaction among functions. For example, after a withdrawal, is it possible to make a deposit? After getting a balance, is it possible to make a deposit?

Remember the basic concept of functional decomposition: we assume the things we are just using (not testing) are perfect, and we worry only about the specific thing we are testing.

For *string*, we're testing the interactions, not the functions that are interacting; so we assume, for example, that *deposit* is perfect. We'll take just a representative sample of the functions we're using to model the function we call *string*. The symbol for representative sample is the parallelogram.

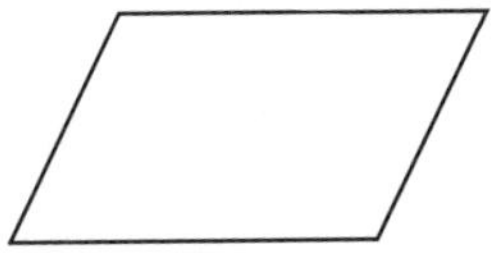

Figure 35: Parallelogram means representative sample

The behavioral model for *string* looks like Figure 36.

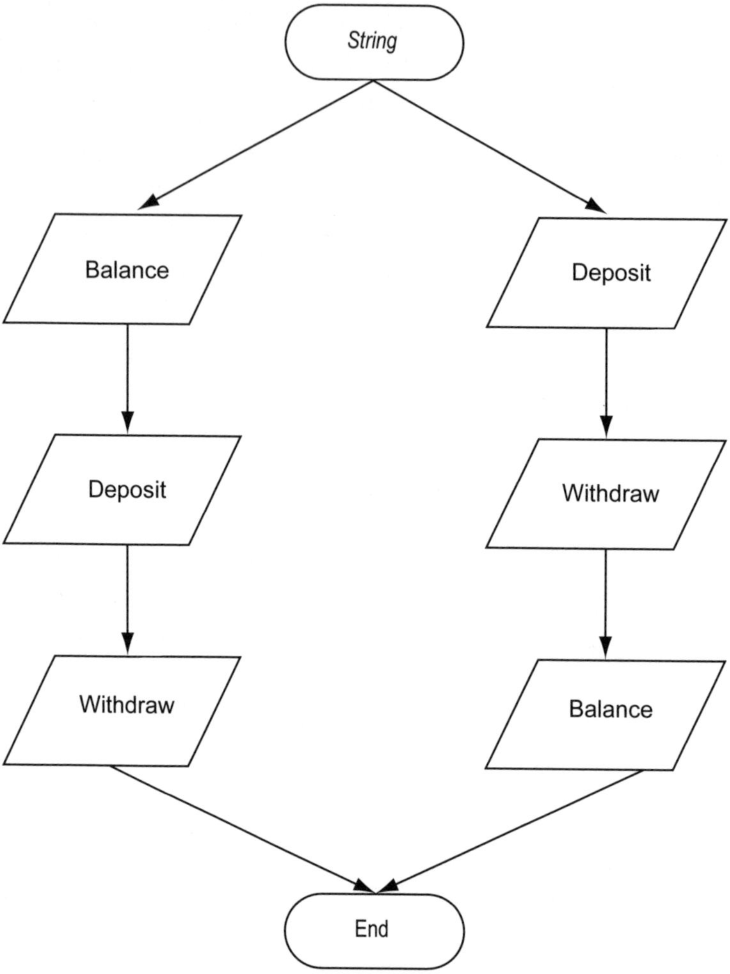

Figure 36: String behavioral model

This model tells us that we don't care what subset of *deposit, withdraw,* or *balance* test cases we choose. We test the details of those functions in other portions of the test suite. Also, we have not listed every combination and permutation of the functions as a part of *string*. How much you list is strictly a judgment call.

The point is to think about it. Do an analysis of what you need, based on your experience, and make the decision that's in the best interest of the project and the users of the AUT.

Weigh the benefit of more testing against the delay in delivering the article to the people who need it.

> Every decision you make in testing is a risk decision, including how much testing you do. Balance the risk of missing a bug against the risk of missing a deadline.

Triangle

Consider this classic example: we'll call it the *triangle* program.

Triangle reads in three values representing the three sides of a triangle. The program determines whether the sides follow triangle rules to form an equilateral, an isosceles, or a scalene triangle.

In an equilateral triangle, all three sides are the same. An isosceles triangle has two sides the same. For purposes of this problem, we will say an isosceles triangle has two and only two sides the same; the third side must be different. A scalene triangle has no sides the same.

One rule of triangles is that the sum of any two sides must be greater than the third side. (This must be true for each of the sides.) After analyzing the values, the program either announces the type of triangle, or, if the inputs do not follow all the rules of triangleness, it announces that it's an improper triangle.

Triangle displays one of four messages:

- Equilateral
- Isosceles
- Scalene
- Improper triangle

How shall we model the behavior of the *triangle* software? Let's ask the basic questions: What does it do? What influences it?

To begin with, the software must distinguish between proper and improper triangles. For the proper triangles, it must determine what type they are. Consider the diagram in Figure 37.

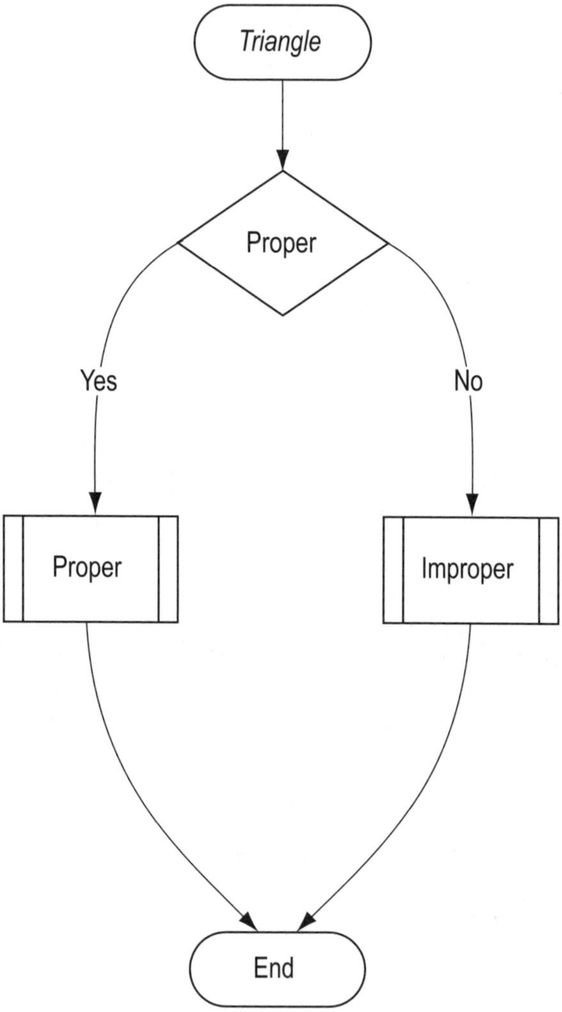

Figure 37: Triangle top-level behavioral model

Our test design will look at both proper and improper triangles. This clearly demonstrates that a behavioral model is *not* a flow chart. It is very unlikely that a software developer would code the *triangle* program as it appears in Figure 37.

When we break down the specification in this way, the lower-level models become quite simple. See Figure 38 and Figure 39.

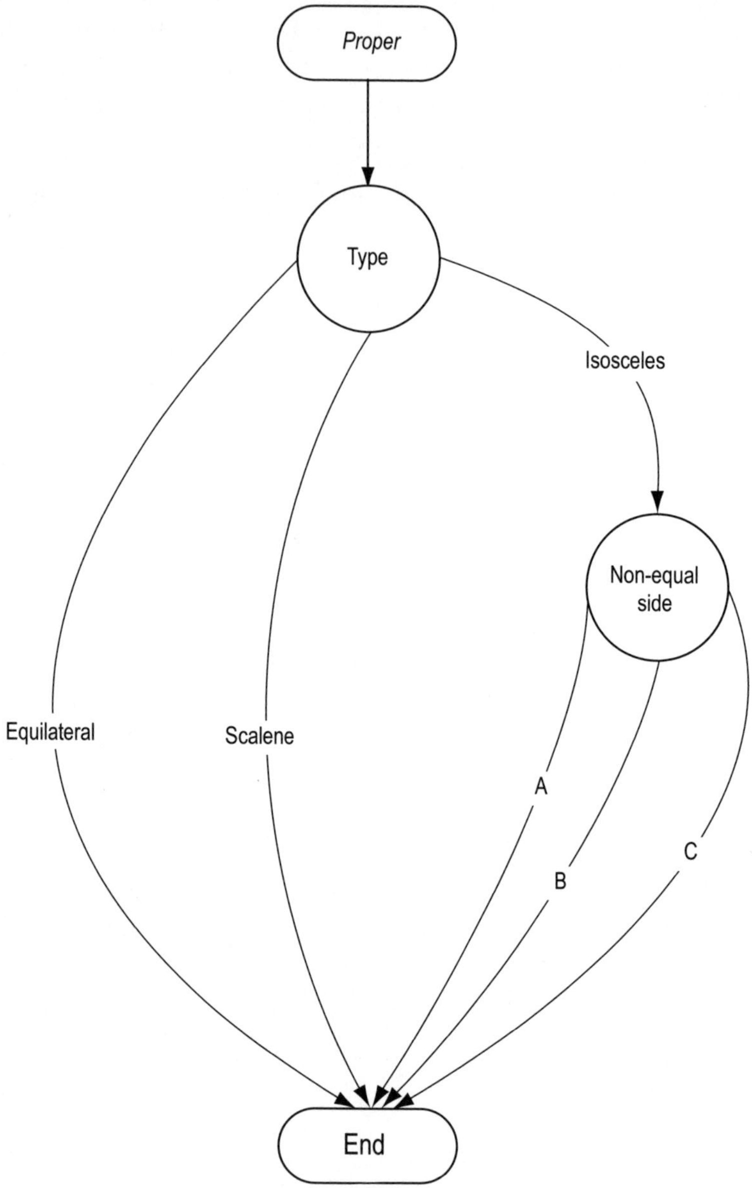

Figure 38: Proper triangle behavioral model

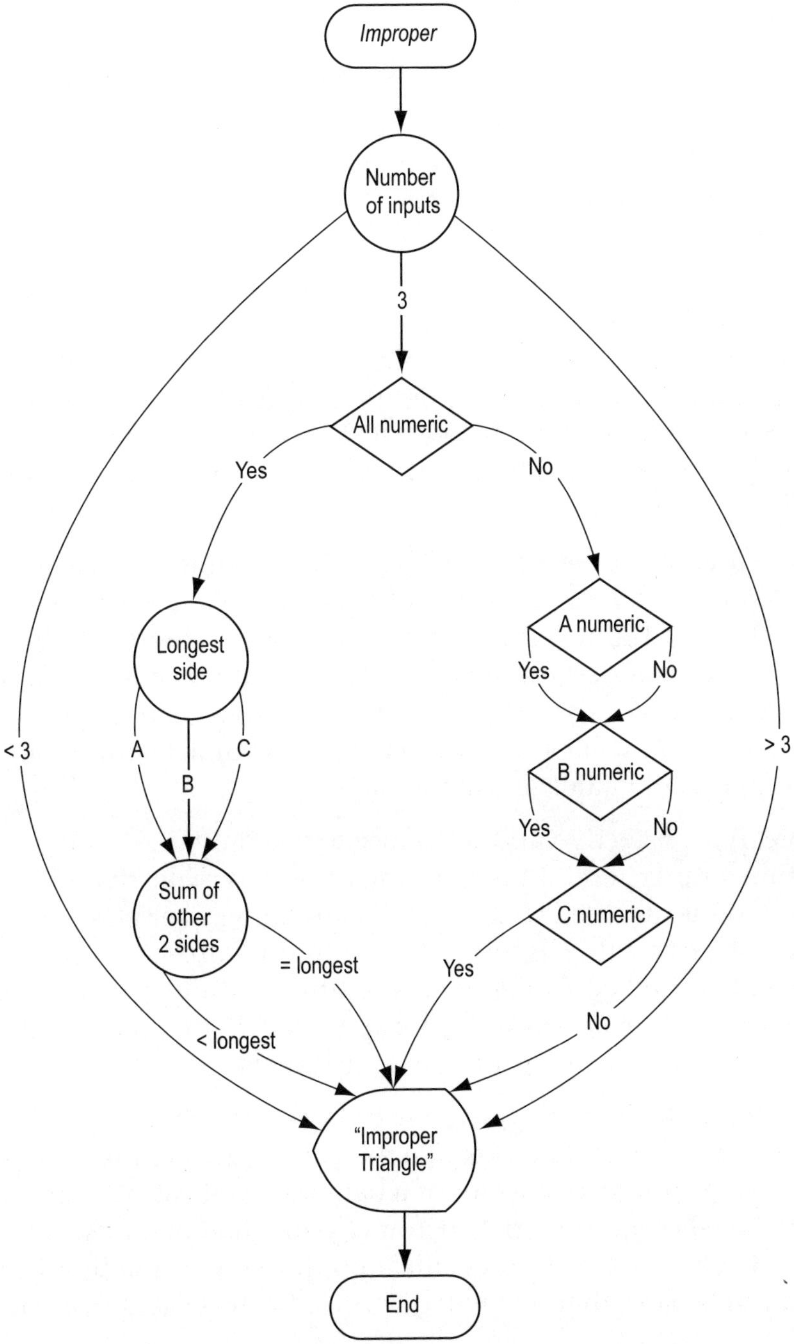

Figure 39: Improper triangle behavioral model

We did not indicate the lengths of the sides in either of the models above. Nor did we, in the *FAST* example or the *bigger* example, indicate any actual values. We don't need to.

An infinite number of possible test cases exists for any program. With our approach, we can describe what a value looks like without worrying about whether the actual length of side of a triangle is 5 or 6 or 167 inches, feet, or miles.

We use the concept of *equivalence partitioning*. For any input parameter or field, we can find a set of equivalence classes. The members of each set are equivalent to all the other members of the set. If this is so, then one input value is all we need for each set. For example, if we choose a test case for equilateral triangles, all we care about is that the sides are equal. We don't care how long the sides are.

There are, of course, some rules about the values for *triangle*. For example, all the sides must be positive. We assume this, even though the specification did not say so. The specification may have bounded the sides by stating that the sides must be within a specific size range. The three equivalence classes for ranges are: all values below the range, all values within the range, and all values above the range.

Note: It is perfectly valid to choose to use only one value within a range, and it takes strong nerves to make that choice! Many of us are used to doing the same thing over and over in our test cases with slightly different input values. If you truly have identified equivalence classes, then testing over and over is wasteful, but we know it's a leap to decide that one number is as good as any other number and run just one.

Another note: Not all equivalence classes are obvious, and sometimes things that look like they are equivalent really are not. For example, one tester of a banking application found a bug that showed up if the customer name had an apostrophe in it. The tester said the specification didn't mention this, but you can be sure that this will be one of his test cases from now on!

While we're on the subject of equivalence partitioning, let's talk about a variant that is sometimes useful: *boundary value analysis*. When the input field is a range of values, instead of picking any value within the range, you can pick the values at each end of the range. Because many coding errors occur at these boundary values, this could be a good way to find them.

Manual Operation

The symbol for a manual operation is shown in Figure 40.

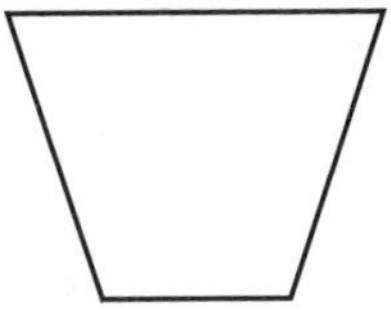

Figure 40: Symbol for manual operation

The purpose of this symbol is to show the tester that he needs to do something — it's a reminder.

When you construct these behavior models, it's important that the model fits on one page. If it does not, go back and look at your functional decomposition. It's possible you need to break down the AUT a bit further.

Should you see something that takes more than one page, it most likely means that the specification is irreducibly complex. Because defects correlate with complexity, the AUT probably needs to be redesigned and not just to make life easier for the tester.

The one-page rule forces us to get down to the simplest component possible.

> The driving notion behind functional decomposition is: Find the simple within the complex.

Rather than decompose the function as far as it would go, in one case, an engineer bent all the lines to make it fit on one page. We have, with permission, reproduced the behavioral model in Figure 41. Most of the text has been removed, but you get the idea.

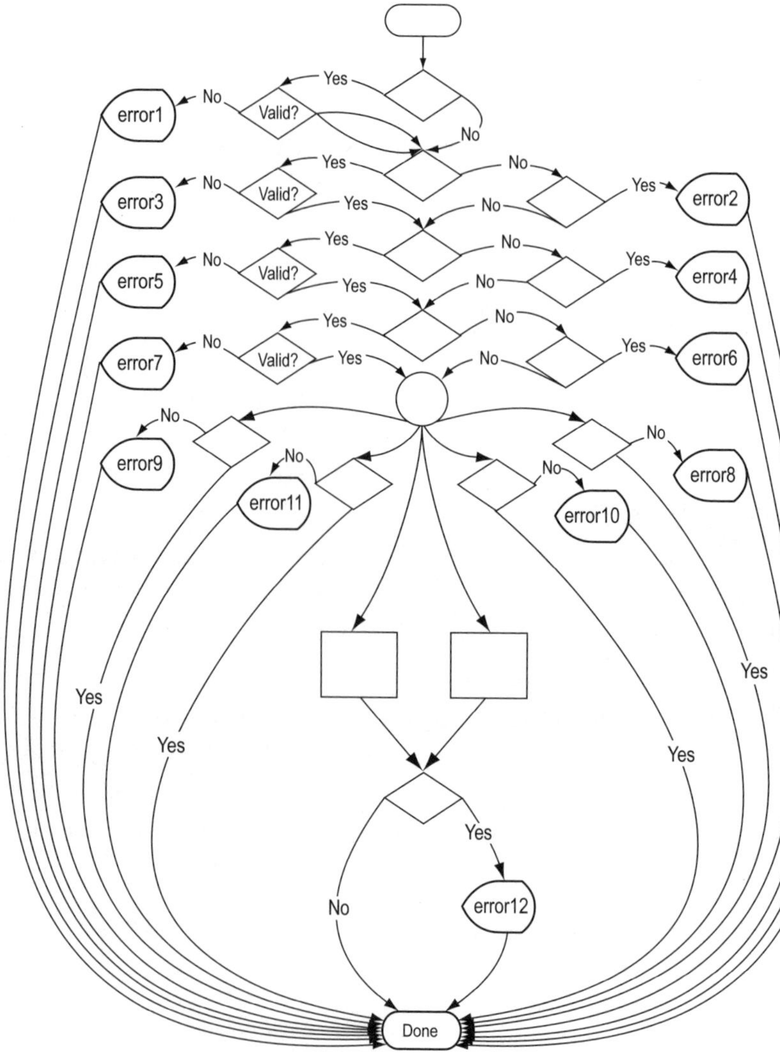

Figure 41: We call this the artichoke

Before we leave the topic of behavioral modeling, it's important to note that we know it seems a simple task to create a behavior model.

We also know it's harder than it looks. The first time you try this on your own, it will be puzzling and frustrating. You may find yourself swearing at whoever wrote the functional specifications for the AUT (or the authors of this book!). The same specs that seemed so clear when you first read them now seem incomplete and ambiguous, and you wonder if they ever were reviewed in the first place.

This is a good thing.

> Your efforts are finding the weaknesses that would sink the project. Be sure to document your findings.

On the other hand, it really is pretty easy to create a behavior model, after you get the hang of it. It just takes practice. Most folks struggle with the first one or two, and then it's smooth sailing. Stick with it. Don't be discouraged.

We've covered behavioral modeling of the test suite. In the next chapter, we'll talk about how to design test cases based on the models.

Chapter 4

Test Case Design: From the Model to the Real Thing

By now, we know that behavioral modeling describes the article under test *as it will behave* when we execute the test suite. Now, we need to design a test suite that implements the behavioral model.

Developers begin with requirements, move down to specification, and move from there into logic design. On the testing side, the process is similar. The behavioral model of the previous section serves as the specification for the test suite. We now move to test case design (TCD).

We need to describe the test suite in a way that shows its totality. If you simply create a list of test cases that state, *do this, do that, now do the other thing,* the result can be a whole lot of pages that are difficult grasp as a part of a larger whole.

We'll lay out TCD on a spreadsheet, using certain conventions. The purpose of those is that the reviewer can see the entire suite at a single glance. Well, maybe a few glances, but you get the idea.

Test Case Design Template

TCD ID:						
Description:						
Author:						
Original Release:			Date:			
Test Case:						
Control Points:						
Expected Results						

Figure 42: TCD template

The top section is called the header. It begins with the identifier for the TCD. Every *TCD ID* is a unique name that helps us locate it in the hierarchy. (We'll talk more about that later.)

The *description* is a brief synopsis of the function to be tested in this TCD. The *author's* name follows. The *original release* refers to the release of the AUT. As follow-on releases introduce changes to the software, it will be helpful to know which test cases may need to change. The *date* tells us when this TCD was completed.

The main body of the TCD is divided into two sections. The left column contains the list of control points. A *control point* is anything you can control or cause. This control-point list is the lowest level of input for individual test cases. (The syntax of control points has a particular nomenclature, which we will talk about as we look at some examples.)

The rest of the main body of the TCD contains a series of columns, each of which represents a test case. Each test case, then, may be thought of as a combination of control points.

The naming of test cases is quite straightforward: Take the name of the TCD and append the number. This is very helpful in complex situations, where the TCD name can tell you exactly where the test cases are in the functional mix.

The final section of the TCD contains the *expected results*. Each column represents a test case. At the bottom of each test case we describe what should occur as a result of executing this particular test case.

Let's look at some examples.

Test Case Design for *Bigger*

Our task now is to translate from the behavior model to the TCD.

Step one is to create the list of control points. All you need to do is locate the decision blocks and case blocks in the behavior model. Each choice in the behavior model translates directly into a control point.

After you create the control point list, start working with the paths indicated in the behavior model. We like to check them off as we go. Remember, there is not necessarily one test case for every path.

For each column in the TCD, predict the outcome and list it in the Expected Results row.

Refer back to the behavior models in Chapter 3 for more information.

Our TCD looks like Figure 43.

TCD ID: B						
Description: Bigger						
Author:						
Original Release: 1.0				Date: 7/5/20xx		
Test case:	B01	B02	B03	B04	B05	B06
Control Points:						
Platform:	*	*	*	*	*	*
Windows	*	*	*	*		
Mac					*	
UNIX						*
Two values input:	*	*	*	*	*	*
no	*					
yes:		*	*	*	*	*
First value numeric?		N	Y	Y	Y	Y
Second value numeric?			N	Y	Y	Y
First number:				*	*	*
bigger than second				*		
equal to second					*	
less than second						*
Expected Results	retrun code = -97	retrun code = -98	retrun code = -99	retrun code = +1	retrun code = 0	retrun code = -1

Figure 43: Bigger TCD

Notice the left column headed Control Points. In this column you see Platform. The line ends with a colon, which tells us that the next several lines are subordinate control points under the main control point, Platform. The subordinate control points are indented. In this case the subordinate control points are the three platforms supported by *bigger*. This means a single test case will only execute on a single platform. The number of levels subordinate control points can have is unlimited. As a general rule, subordinate control points at the lowest level are mutually exclusive.

In the body of the TCD, you'll see mostly blank cells or cells filled with asterisks. The asterisk tells us that something is chosen or exists. For example, under Platform, Windows is selected in some of the cells or columns but not in others. This tells us that we'll execute the test case on the Windows platform for those test cases where Windows is chosen. The asterisk is merely the existence operator.

Now notice the line that says "First value numeric?" The ? tells us that, just as in any other writing, this is a question. It is answered either Y for yes or N for no.

Another symbol that often appears in TCDs, although not in this example, is the equal sign. For example, had we chosen to specify an actual value for the inputs, we could have put "value =" in the left column and filled in the actual value in the cell for each particular test case. We've chosen not to do that here; rather, we specify the actual value later.

Now, look at the last row in the TCD. Here we specify the expected results of the test case execution. The formatting, you'll notice, is sideways. This allows it to be readable and gives you more room for the information you're going to need.

This small example demonstrates some of the power of TCDs. You can simply look at the TCD, notice the pattern in the cells, and determine whether you have adequate coverage. For example, if there are very few asterisks in an area, then there may be too few test cases. (Unfortunately, this is one of those sentences that will make more sense after you have created a few of these TCDs. Be patient — it is an important concept, because coverage really is one of the primary issues in test design.)

> We always need to know that we sufficiently cover the functionality of the AUT.

These TCDs allow us to determine if we have or have not done so.

Congratulations! You have completed your first TCD. Okay, so you did not actually do it; we led you down the path. But surely you followed along closely enough to deserve congratulations. When you strike out on your own, it may seem a bit difficult at first; but keep in mind that this will be your first attempt.

Bigger is really quite simple. More complex applications can take quite a long time to analyze. In planning your project, you should consider how long creating a TCD takes. The range, depending on complexity and size of the AUT, could be from a few hours to several weeks.

Our one-page rule for behavioral models applies to the TCD as well. The TCD must fit on one page if you were to print it. And, yes, sometimes we use a small font to make it fit!

Test Case Design for *FAST*

So far, we have seen an example of a single-level TCD. These are little to no help for most applications. We use the process of functional decomposition to break up the AUT into manageable units, which is reflected in the behavior models we have already seen. For an example, see Figure 19 in Chapter 3.

How do we show this in a TCD? The template in Figure 44 will help.

TCD ID:		
Description:		
Author:		
Original Release:		Date:
Function:	**TCD:**	**Page:**

Figure 44: High-level TCD template

In this high-level TCD template, we show the hierarchical structure of the AUT. The first column has changed. We no longer think of control points; rather, we think of functions.

The next column is headed TCD, which stands for test case design. Here, we list the identifier for the next level TCD. That next level may be another high-level TCD, or it may be the lowest-level TCD. This drilling down can go to several levels. We recommend using no more than six.

The third column is for the page number. This may or may not be valuable in your setting. If all of your work is electronic, you don't need the page number; you simply hyperlink from the TCD column to where you want go. In some environments, the TCD is printed, and the page number reference helps someone trying to find his or her way through the document. Keep in mind that these documents can get fairly involved and very long, so anything that helps the reader is useful.

The high-level TCD for *FAST* is shown in Figure 45.

TCD ID: F
Description: FAST
Author:
Original Release: 1.0 **Date:** 9/7/20xx

Function:	TCD:	Page:
Balance	FB	
Deposit	FD	
Exceptions	FE	
Sign on	FS	
Transfer	FT	
Withdraw	FW	
String	FR	

Figure 45: FAST high-level TCD

Each of the lower-level TCDs is referred to by a name. The name begins with the ID of the current TCD and adds a character that indicates the next level functionality. After you do the initial functional decomposition, this approach allows you to assign different pieces of the application to different members of the team.

The good news is this: We now know exactly what the test suite looks like. The bad news? We now must implement the TCD.

Let's look at a couple of the lower-level TCDs. Figure 46 shows the *deposit* function from *FAST.*

Matrix ID:	**FD**					
Description:	**FAST Deposit**					
Author:						
Original Release:	**1.0**			**Date:**	**######**	
Test case:	FD01	FD02	FD03	FD04	FD05	FD06
Control Points:						
To Account:	*	*	*	*	*	*
Checking	*	*	*			
Savings				*	*	*
Account exists?	N	Y	Y	N	Y	Y
Amount of deposit:		*	*		*	*
valid			*			*
invalid		*			*	
Expected Results	"Requested Account Does Not Exist. Re-enter."	"Invalid amount. Re-enter." Re-entered amount accepted.	Account balance updated with the deposited amount.	"Requested Account Does Not Exist. Re-enter."	"Invalid amount. Re-enter."	Account balance updated with the deposited amount.

Figure 46: FAST deposit TCD

One of the control points is "To Account." The subordinate control points are Checking and Savings accounts. In the "Account exists?" line, the ? tells us that this is a question to be answered as either Y or N. Another way to say exactly the same thing is this:

Account Exists:
Yes
No

With this form, asterisks in the appropriate cells give the reader the needed information. You'll see an example of this a bit later.

Why would you use one format over the other? The answer depends on what you're trying to communicate to the reader of the TCD. Using the second form above often shows more emphasis on the choice to be made.

Now, let's look at the TCD for the *withdraw* function of *FAST* in Figure 47.

Matrix ID:	**FW**									
Description:	**FAST Withdraw**									
Author:										
Original Release:	**1.0**			**Date:**	**######**					
Test case:	FW01	FW02	FW03	FW04	FW05	FW06	FW07	FW08	FW09	FW10
Control Points:										
From Account:	*	*	*	*	*	*	*	*	*	*
Checking	*		*	*	*	*				
Savings		*					*	*	*	*
From Account exists?	N	N	Y	Y	Y	Y	Y	Y	Y	Y
Amount of withdrawal:			*	*	*	*	*	*	*	*
zero			*				*			
more than in "from"				*				*		
Multiple of $20?					Y	Y			Y	Y
More than in FAST?					Y	N			Y	N
Expected Results	"From Account Does Not Exist"		"Cannot withdraw zero."	"Insufficient funds in From Account. Re-enter or cancel."	"Not enough cash to service your request. Re-enter or cancel."	Cash dispensed. Amount deducted from account.	"Cannot withdraw zero."	"Insufficient funds in From Account. Re-enter or cancel."	"Not enough cash to service your request. Re-enter or cancel."	Cash dispensed. Amount deducted from account.

Figure 47: FAST withdraw TCD

In the examples so far, each test case ended with a single column describing the expected results. In the *withdraw* example in Figure 47, we see two adjacent test cases that have exactly the same expected result. When this happens, we combine the expected results cells into one.

This concept can be very interesting. What if you have three adjacent columns that have some results the same in all three, some results the same in two of the three, and some results unique to each individual test case. In this case, the Expected Results row would look like Figure 48.

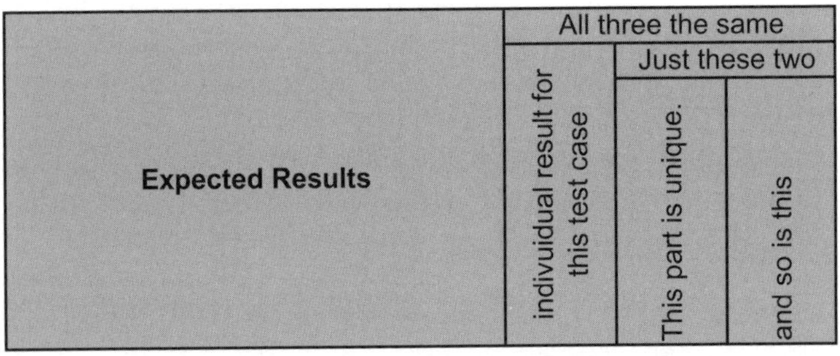

Figure 48: Expected results for complex outcomes

To see how all this plays together, look at Appendix E, which contains the entire TCD for *FAST*.

Test Case Design for *Triangle*

These next few pages will show the TCD for *triangle*. As a reference, you may want to review the behavior models in Chapter 3.

TCD ID: T		
Description: High order test design for triangle		
Author:		
Original Release: 1.0 Date: 6/5/20xx		
Function:	**TCD:**	**Page:**
Improper	TI	
Proper	TP	

Figure 49: Triangle TCD

Description: Triangle; Improper triangles									
Author:									
Original Release: 1.0					**Date:** 7/5/20xx				
Test case:	TI 01	TI 02	TI 03	TI 04	TI 05	TI 06	TI 07	TI 08	TI 09
Control Points:									
Number of inputs:	*	*	*	*	*	*	*	*	*
<3	*								
>3		*							
=3			*	*	*	*	*	*	*
All input numeric:			*	*	*	*	*	*	*
yes:			*	*	*				
Longest side=			A	B	C				
Sum of other two sides:			*	*	*				
= longest			*						
< longest				*	*				
no:						*	*	*	*
A numeric?						N	Y	Y	N
B numeric?						N	Y	N	N
C numeric?						N	N	Y	Y
Expected Results	All test cases result in the message "Improper Triangle"								

Figure 50: Triangle - improper TCD

TCD ID:	TP				
Description:	Triangle; Proper triangles				
Author:					
Original Release:	1.0			Date: 7/5/20xx	
Test case:	TP 01	TP 02	TP 03	TP 04	TP 05
Control Points:					
type of triangle:	*	*	*	*	*
equilateral	*				
scalene		*			
isosceles:			*	*	*
short side=			A	B	C
Expected Results	Equilateral	Scalene	Isosceles		

Figure 51: Triangle - proper TCD

In this chapter, we have translated the behavioral models into TCDs.

Consider the process. Most of our creativity is spent in the model. Creating the TCDs should take far less creativity and thought. The TCD describes what to include in each test case.

When you script the test cases, even less thought should be required. The only question left is how you will actually execute the test. The pattern repeats, in that the ideal is to reduce the necessary thought to zero for executing the test cases. That's why turning them over to a test tool can be so effective. Test automation is most successful if the test suite is well designed.

In the next chapter, we'll explore ways to optimize testing, including test automation, business impact testing, test frameworks, change impact testing, and the important topic of knowing how much to automate.

Chapter 5

Test Optimization: Balancing Risk and Effort

In our view, testing is not just about finding defects and improving the quality of a product.

Test teams are never given enough time to perform all the rigors of testing, so they end up finding a balance between an acceptable defect rate and the investment necessary to get to that point. There are several ways to find that balance.

Our approach is always to take a business perspective and attempt to bridge the gap between business and IT. Because we believe that the business, with input from the testing team, should define the quality levels needed for a smooth operation, we've developed a test optimization approach called Business Impact Testing.

In this chapter, we'll explain how it works.

First, we analyze the business risk. Then, based on that risk, we can make specific decisions to optimize testing.

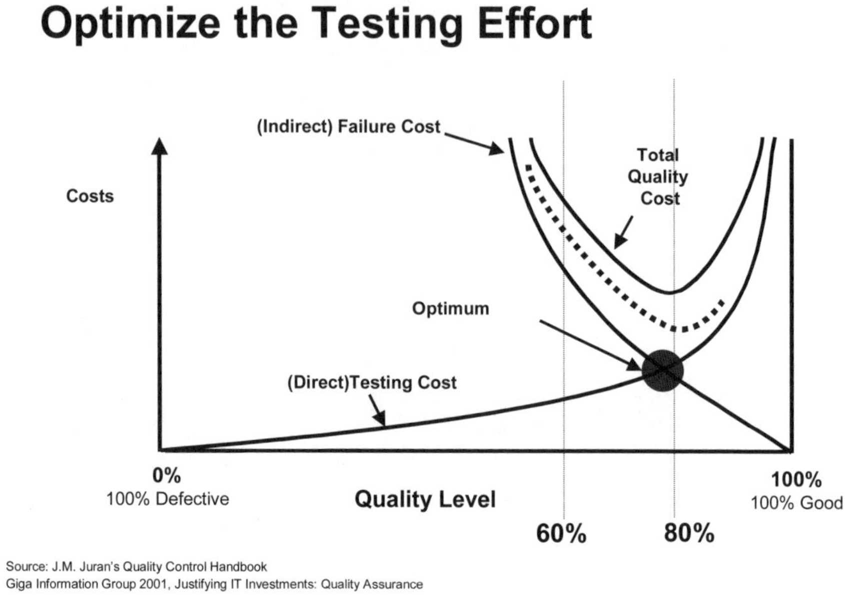

Figure 52: Diminishing returns of testing, finding the optimum point, and balancing risk and effort

The basic elements for our risk assessment are the business functions we obtain from the functional breakdown described in Chapter 2. We'll assess each of the business functions using a standardized approach.

The Business Impact Testing approach in the Mercury Quality Model follows these steps:

1. Assess the business impact of each business function.
2. Assess the probability of failure for each business function.
3. Derive the business risk from the result of these assessments.
4. Define the test procedure to apply for each risk level.
5. Assess the functional complexity of the business functions.
6. Calculate the effort for testing.

7. Balance the effort between automation and manual test execution based on the given parameters of your environment.
8. Adapt testing frameworks and leverage change impact to optimize testing effort.

Risk Assessment

In software, a risk threatens one or more of the functions the software is expected to perform and has an uncertain probability of occurring. We typically describe risk as a result of the probability that a failure will occur and the expected damage the failure can cause if it does occur.

Another way to see this is in this formula:

> Risk = damage caused by a failure X the probability the failure will happen

It's important to remember that the formula helps us understand the magnitude of the risk, but it does not help us cope with the uncertainty.

> We can calculate risk, but we can only estimate uncertainty. This exercise is more about comparison than accuracy.

Our approach uses this risk definition as a basis for our risk model — we built a model to assess risk in a very pragmatic way that requires only solid knowledge of the business and a good understanding of the system design. (We've seen some very complicated models that have not been successful in the field because they're too difficult to adopt and too technical.

The learning curve of these risk models quickly increases the cost of testing and does not speak a business language.)

We want a risk model that's easy to understand and implement, but still gives us enough information to allow maximum test optimization.

Because our whole approach is about risk mitigation at a reasonable cost, we conduct the risk assessment to achieve the following goals:

- Transparency of the functionality under test
- Focus on business-critical functions
- Knowledge of the test coverage

If we use the result of the functional breakdown and assess each business function, we'll achieve those goals.

We assign the functionality with the highest business risk the highest priority, and we determine the effort to expend and which test activities to undertake for a single business function based on the prioritization of risk.

> To calculate business risk, we need to determine the damage we would expect from a failure and the probability of the failure to occur.

As a result, we conduct our risk assessment in two phases.

First, we assess the impact to the business of each business function. *Impact* in this context means to what extent we need the functionality in order to perform the business' day-to-day operations, or how much damage a failure of the function will cause to the business.

Second, we look at the probability that a defect will occur in the assessed business function.

After we have completed these two steps, we'll derive the risk for each business function as a result of both values.

Business Impact Analysis

First, we conduct the business impact analysis for all business functions that belong to the application under test. We use criteria that are common for all business units so the results are comparable throughout the enterprise.

Business impact criteria are defined in terms of the damage to the business if a failure were to occur (Figure 53).

Criteria	Result		
	a High Impact	b Medium Impact	c Low Impact
Type of process	calculation / validation	change of data	display
Business implication	legal	wrong information	none
Frequency of use	very often	often	rare
Number of customers affected	large number / very important	group	some

Figure 53: Sample business impact analysis

We've based this information on many successful implementations where it has proven sufficient and practical. We can change or adapt the criteria of course, depending on the individual situation in a given environment.

During the assessment, we check each business function against each criterion. The result of the analysis allows us to categorize all the business functions into three business impact categories: high, medium, and low.

We determine the impact using a formula agreed upon by the business and testing team.

For the example in Figure 53, we might use the following formula:

- **High impact** — Any business function with two or more high-impact criteria; or two or more medium-impact criteria and one criteria with high impact.
- **Medium impact** — Any business function with two or more medium-impact criteria and none with high impact; or one high-impact criteria, one with medium impact, and all other criteria with low impact.
- **Low impact** — Any other combinations.

This is of course just an example and we would modify this formula for different situations.

Note: In the Mercury release of Quality Center 9.0 and higher, the entire business risk analysis has been automated. For more information, contact a Mercury representative.

Failure Probability

Like the business impact, the failure probability is the result of an assessment based on criteria that should be standard for the whole company (Figure 54).

Criteria	Result		
	III Unlikely	II Likely	I Very Likely
Change rate	unchanged	changed function	new function
Software maturity	mature (> 10 years)	progressing (5 -10 years)	immature (< 5 years)
Defect rate	low	medium	high

Figure 54: Failure probability

Depending on a given environment, we can change and adapt the criteria.

During the assessment, each business function is checked with each criterion. Again, we can categorize business functions into three probability categories: very likely, likely, and unlikely.

We determine the impact from an agreed upon formula. Using the example in the table above, we might apply the following formula:

- **Very likely** — Any business function with two or more criteria that are very likely to occur; or two or more criteria that are likely and one criterion that is very likely to occur.
- **Likely** — Any business function with two or more criteria likely to occur and none that is very likely to occur; or one criteria very likely to occur, one likely to occur, and all other criteria being unlikely to occur.
- **Unlikely** — Any other combinations.

After we have completed the assessment and have a value for the impact and the probability, we make the final step to derive the final business risk.

Derive Business Risk

We calculate the risk based on the combined results of the business impact analysis and the failure probability assessment. The combination allows us to finally categorize the business functions in terms of high risk, medium risk, or low risk (Figure 55).

Impact	Probability		
	III Unlikely	II Likely	I Very Likely
a High impact	Medium risk	High risk	High risk
b Medium impact	Low risk	Medium risk	Medium risk
c Low impact	Low risk	Low risk	Medium risk

Figure 55: Calculating risk categories

After we've calculated the risk, we can design the test procedure to be applied during integration testing for the business function.

Test Procedure Definition

We define different test procedures for each risk level with the risk analysis information.

> The key is to invest testing resources according to the priority of risk.

A test procedure lays out the test strategy we'll apply in order to:

- Define the test approach.
- Select the test data.
- Set the test optimization level (using automation, business process frameworks, or other test strategies).

We typically devise an effective test procedure from a combination of experience and mathematical calculations. To keep things simple for now, we only show the test procedure example based on our experiences (Figure 56). (We'll discuss how to determine the optimum mix between automation and manual testing later in this chapter.)

Test Procedures

Approach based on Risk

Procedure for High Risk	Procedure	Systematic testing using business component testing strategy, and root-cause analysis
	Approach	Automate 30% with business process testing Framework, Manual test 70%, leverage change
Procedure for Medium Risk	Procedure	Systematic testing with or without business component testing strategy, and root-cause analysis
	Approach	Use traditional automation 20%, manual 80%
Procedure for Low Risk	Procedure	Systematic or ad-hoc testing
	Approach	Automated: 5% Manual: 95%, outsource testing

Figure 56: Sample test procedures

Adapt the test procedure to the specific needs of the business the application is written for.

Functional Complexity

Next, we assess the functional complexity of each business function to estimate the effort we should budget for the testing activities.

> Being able to estimate testing efforts allows us to better plan the software testing life cycle, align resources, and leverage test strategies and technology.

We know that functions involving a large number of assets, such as data sets, interfaces, or components, take more time to test than a function that involves only a few assets. Each test requires preliminary activities, such as test case development, data preparation, and test result evaluation.

After we complete the risk assessment and define the test procedure for each risk class, we've laid the foundation to estimate the test effort. But we need to know the functional complexity of the business function.

Functional complexity analysis indicates the amount of testing development effort we expect to go into the business function. More complex requirements lead to a more complex implementation that is more error prone and thus needs more testing.

From a testing point of view, the functional complexity depends on the number of objects or assets involved in the business function. Objects, in this case, do not refer to an object-oriented approach, but rather to all kinds of assets, such as tables, data sets, forms, and templates. The tester has to prepare and evaluate the data for each such object (Figure 57).

Criteria	Result		
	1 High Complexity	2 Medium Complexity	3 Low Complexity
Number of objects affected	>9	4-9	<4
Number of objects with write access	>3	1-3	<1
Number of objects with read access	>5	3-5	<3
Number of windows affected	>4	2-4	<2

Figure 57: Functional complexity

As in the risk assessment, we'll assess all business functions against each criterion. We'll derive the results using the following rules:

- **Risk class 1** — A business function rated 1 at least twice; or 1 once and 2 at least twice.
- **Risk class 2** — A business function rated 2 at least twice; or 1 once and 2 once.
- **Risk class 3** — All other cases.

Test Effort Estimation

Starting with the effort each business function requires, and depending on the test procedure we've defined and the functional complexity, we can make test effort estimations.

Based on many projects, we've built a test effort baseline model that organizations can use when its own numbers are not available.

The following matrix shows the effort that has to be spent in integration testing to execute the respective test procedures. (The numbers come from projects delivered in the past five years.)

Test Effort for Integration Test

Not Optimized

	1 High Complexity	2 Medium Complexity	3 Low Complexity	Test Procedure
A High Risk	13 - 19	10 – 16	7- 13	Procedure for High Risk
B Medium Risk	6.5 – 9.5	6.5 – 9.5	4 – 6.5	Procedure for Medium Risk
C Low Risk	2.3	2.2	1.2 – 2.2	Procedure for Low Risk

Effort in FTEs for Test Case development, Test Data definition, Test Script development, Test execution and Test evaluation per Business Function

To get a better understanding of how much work goes into which activity, we have broken down the overall effort into the different activities:

1. Develop test cases for the high- and medium-risk business functions, using the behavioral modeling described in Chapter 3.

Test Case Development Effort

	1 High Complexity	2 Medium Complexity	3 Low Complexity	Test Procedure
A High Risk	4 - 6	3 – 5	2- 4	Procedure for High Risk
B Medium Risk	2 - 3	2 - 3	1 – 2	Procedure for Medium Risk
C Low Risk	1	1	0.5 - 1	Procedure for Low Risk

Effort in FTEs for
Test Case development per Business Function

2. Develop or define the test data by completing two tasks.

   First, we have to define the test data that goes into the test rule. Second, we have to define the test data that must be in the system to serve as the data environment for the test case. For example, if the test case is about to close an account, this account has to be in the system and open to make sure the test case leads to a positive result.

Test Data Development Effort

	1 High Complexity	2 Medium Complexity	3 Low Complexity	Test Procedure
A High Risk	4 - 6	3 – 5	2- 4	Procedure for High Risk
B Medium Risk	2 - 3	2 - 3	1 – 2	Procedure for Medium Risk
C Low Risk	1	1	0.5 - 1	Procedure for Low Risk

Effort in FTEs for Test Data development per Business Function

3. Create the test scripts for automation. We start with a fairly low amount of test automation, like 30 percent for high-risk business functions and 20 percent for medium-risk business functions. But even this low amount of automation takes some effort.

Test Script Development Effort

	1 High Complexity	2 Medium Complexity	3 Low Complexity	Test Procedure
A High Risk	2 - 3	1 – 2	1- 2	Procedure for High Risk
B Medium Risk	1	1	0.5 - 1	Procedure for Medium Risk
C Low Risk	n.a.	n.a.	n.a.	Procedure for Low Risk

Effort in FTEs for Test Script development per Business Function

4. Apply the test evaluation effort only for the test cases we're automating — for manual test cases, the evaluation takes place during the execution.

Test Evaluation Effort

	1 High Complexity	2 Medium Complexity	3 Low Complexity	Test Procedure
A High Risk	2 - 3	2 - 3	1 - 2	Procedure for High Risk
B Medium Risk	1 - 2	1 - 2	1	Procedure for Medium Risk
C Low Risk	0	0	0	Procedure for Low Risk

Effort in FTEs for
Test Evaluation per Business Function

5. Estimate the effort for one manual test execution. Each test case, whether or not it will be automated, is usually executed at least once manually as a best practice.

Manual Test Execution Effort

	1 High Complexity	2 Medium Complexity	3 Low Complexity	Test Procedure
A High Risk	1	1	1	Procedure for High Risk
B Medium Risk	0.5	0.5	0.5	Procedure for Medium Risk
C Low Risk	0.3	0.2	0.2	Procedure for Low Risk

Effort in FTEs for
Manual Test Execution per Business Function

By taking the business-impact approach, we make sure to concentrate the test activities on the most critical business functions.

How to Calculate the Optimal Level of Automation

Examining the effort for the different activities inevitably brings up the question of what level of test automation is the optimum from a cost-value ratio. Using the same sample scenario from above, we compare the additional effort required for automation to a single complete manual test cycle per risk class.

Additional Effort for Automation

	1 High Complexity	2 Medium Complexity	3 Low Complexity	Test Procedure
A High Risk	1.5 – 2.5	0.5 – 1.5	0.5 – 1.5	Procedure for High Risk
B Medium Risk	0.25	0.25	0 – 0.25	Procedure for Medium Risk
C Low Risk	0	0	0	Procedure for Low Risk

Additional Effort in FTEs for Test automation compared to Manual test execution per Business Function

This chart represents the extra effort or investment required for automation compared to a complete manual test.

In the next chart, which shows the second step, we're looking at the savings we achieve through automation for each test cycle after the initial investment of effort to automate the test.

Effort Saved through Automation

	1 High Complexity	2 Medium Complexity	3 Low Complexity	Test Procedure
A High Risk	0.5	0.5	0.5	Procedure for High Risk
B Medium Risk	0.25	0.25	0.25	Procedure for Medium Risk
C Low Risk	0	0	0	Procedure for Low Risk

Effort in FTEs for One Test Cycle per Business Function

The calculated savings over time would allow automated tests to break even with manual tests after a few test cycles depending on test automation level.

Number of Cycles Needed to Break Even

	1 High Complexity	2 Medium Complexity	3 Low Complexity	Test Procedure
A High Risk	3 - 5	1 - 3	1 – 3	Procedure for High Risk
B Medium Risk	1	1	0 – 1	Procedure for Medium Risk
C Low Risk	0	0	0	Procedure for Low Risk

Additional Effort in FTEs for Test automation compared to Manual test execution per Business Function

The higher the complexity and risk, the more cycles are needed in order to break even.

Now, let's look at the same figures with a higher percentage of automation. We're assuming that we automate all test cases.

The additional effort would be as shown in the next chart.

Additional Effort for Automation

	1 High Complexity	2 Medium Complexity	3 Low Complexity	Test Procedure
A High Risk	5.5 – 8.5	1.5 – 5.5	1.5 – 5.5	100 % Automation
B Medium Risk	2.25	2.25	1- 2.25	100 % Automation
C Low Risk	0	0	0	Manual

Additional Effort in FTEs for Test automation compared to Manual test execution per Business Function

Based on those figures, the savings for each test cycle after the initial test cycle is shown in the next chart.

Effort Saved through Automation

	1 High Complexity	2 Medium Complexity	3 Low Complexity	Test Procedure
A High Risk	1.5	1.5	1.5	100 % Automation
B Medium Risk	0.75	0.75	0.75	100 % Automation
C Low Risk	0	0	0	Procedure for Low Risk

Effort in FTEs for One Test Cycle per Business Function

This leads to the following number of test cycles that would allow us to break even.

Number of Cycles Needed to Break Even

	1 High Complexity	2 Medium Complexity	3 Low Complexity	Test Procedure
A High Risk	3 - 5	1 - 3	1 – 3	100% Automation
B Medium Risk	2 - 3	2 - 3	1 - 3	100% Automation
C Low Risk	0	0	0	Procedure for Low Risk

Looking at the total picture, it becomes clear that the number of cycles needed to break even goes up and we assume it's possible to handle the challenges with the test data.

Remember that these sample numbers are a best-case scenario, assuming we're following the proper business impact testing strategies, using the best traditional automation solutions, and employing expert test automation engineers.

In most organizations, the test cycles required for test automation to break even with manual testing can be much higher. It's very important to do these calculations for your specific environment to get to your optimum test automation levels. Generally, 30 to 50 percent test automation has proven to be the optimum level for most situations using traditional test automation techniques. In the next section, we introduce a couple of new concepts that can significantly improve the return on investment and efficiencies of test automation.

Test Effort Optimization

Looking at the different activities that need to be performed to a complete testing, we've isolated some areas where efficiency can be improved.

Improving Test Automation and Manual Testing

The points below show us why test automation can increase an organization's testing efficiencies; however, the extra investment and existing organizational skill sets often make this adoption slow. To make test automation feasible, we need to combine traditional technological approaches with business-oriented testing frameworks.

- Automation can drastically reduce the effort needed for regression testing.
- Automation can enable last-minute sanity checks during fast-change cycles when it's impossible to test manually because of time constraints.
- Automation enables consistency and logic coverage. There is no risk that test cases are left out or errors are overlooked if they are designed correctly.
- Automation gives the option for a higher regression rate because only computing time is involved when running the test.

To achieve these improvements, we can leverage a combination of new testing frameworks and new testing technologies. Let's examine a couple of the most interesting and profound of these improvements.

Over the past years, several improvements have made testing more efficient, and the latest comes from the business process testing framework (Figure 58).

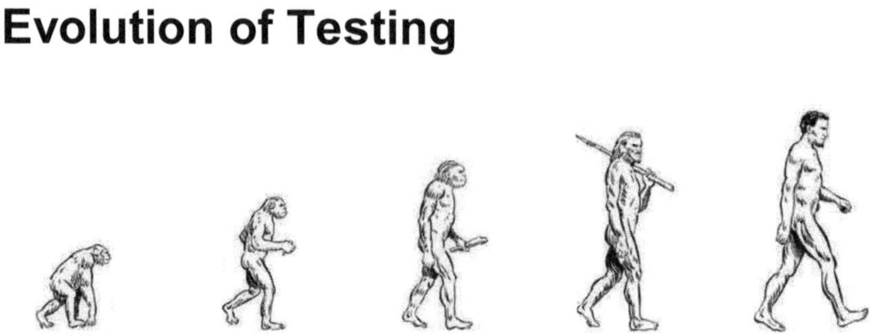

Unsupported Manual Functional Testing	Tool Supported Manual Functional Testing	Automated Functional Testing	Custom Test Automation Framework	Business Process Testing
• Inefficient • Ineffective • Inconsistent • Incomprehensive	Though to a lesser degree.	• Technically complicated • Depends on application availability and stability • High maintenance costs • Documentation separate from automation	• Very technically complicated • Difficult and expensive to design, develop, and maintain • Tendency towards narrow focus • Possibility of breaking between Mercury product releases • Not your core competency	• Buy versus build • Start where everyone else stops • Get more functionality faster • Supported across more applications in more environments • Won't break between Mercury product releases • Delivers this value...
• Disconnected • Inaccessible • Indecisive • Not reusable				

Figure 58: Five generations of testing improvements

Business Process Testing™ (BPT) is one of the most profound and revolutionary new test frameworks for optimizing testing today. But to fully understand the benefits and appreciate the value of this approach, we must first understand the history of software testing over the past 15 to 20 years.

Manual testing was originally the only method of software testing. A lead tester would typically design the test cases and, if you were lucky, you got a printed sheet of paper with instructions on how to navigate the software and hints about the results you should expect to see when you navigated the software.

Testing was mostly ad-hoc and inconsistent, and test coverage was poor.

Automated software testing was invented to address these issues. Although the concept of automated software testing has been around for quite some time, it's still being adopted only reluctantly in many organizations. As a matter of fact, based on what we see in the industry, about 80 percent of software applications are still tested manually.

Automated software testing advancements have come a long way in a short time. Each successive generation of solutions has handled more significant challenges, yet each advance has introduced a new set of issues to be resolved.

First-generation products, introduced about 15 years ago, were hardware-based capture/playback systems, like macros that recorded keystrokes and replayed them on demand. These tests were easy to create, but they had limited validations and checkpoints, and they were difficult to maintain and document as changes occurred.

Second-generation solutions appeared about 10 years ago — software-based capture/playback systems that recorded test cases and represented them as scripts. This approach gave us wider test coverage and more robust checkpoints and validations, but required specialized development skills and did not completely solve the maintenance challenge. Every time an application changed, the test scripts had to be updated, which meant modifications to many lines of code and continual documentation updates to reflect these changes.

Third-generation automated testing solutions, called "test frameworks," have been on the market since 2001. Test frameworks added a layer of abstraction over the scripting process so non-technical people could build tests.

With this approach, subject matter experts (SMEs or business analysts) could draw on a library of prebuilt "keywords," which implemented a specific action against the application (for example, "click the OK button"). Keywords made it possible to develop automated test cases with no procedural programming experience.

Test frameworks led to dramatic productivity increases for many software testing teams, but they still had many shortcomings. For example:

- The operations performed by any particular keyword tended to be very fine-grained or atomic. Designing a test for an entire business process required hundreds of individual keywords, which is a time-consuming process.
- Because test framework solutions consist of files with keywords and their associated data elements, SMEs found they were still creating scripts, despite promises of "scriptless test design."
- Traditional test framework products were not always backward compatible with previous-generation technology (such as recorders), which limited their flexibility and power. Test engineers couldn't get under the hood and modify the code underlying the keywords even if they wanted to.
- Test frameworks and keyword-based products still didn't function at the business process level, which forced SMEs to think like programmers and constrained adoption rates.
- Test frameworks did not help create test documentation, and therefore many man-hours were needed to assemble the detailed information required for compliance with several legislative acts that regulate data access, including Sarbanes Oxley and the Health Information Portability and Accountability Act (HIPAA).

It was clear that a simple modification or enhancement to previous generation software testing solutions would continue to solve some problems, but cause others.

We needed a revolutionary approach that could radically streamline test design, test automation, test maintenance, and the expensive and time-consuming test documentation processes. The latest generation of testing solutions was built on the experiences of the previous 15 years.

> Business Process Testing is the first complete role-based test framework to bridge the quality chasm by enabling business analysts and quality engineers to collaborate effectively.

The Business Process Testing framework enables nontechnical SMEs to build, data-drive, execute, and document test steps without deep technical knowledge. They can create high-level test flows that mirror actual business processes, which frees quality engineers to concentrate their efforts on areas that facilitate automation.

The benefits of Business Process Testing far surpass any of the previous generation of testing solutions:

- It greatly simplifies and speeds up the test-design process by using components (business-process building blocks).
- It allows QA and testing teams to start the test-design process much sooner — during system design — which accelerates time to deployment for high-quality software.
- It generates automated tests and test-case documentation in a *single step*, which eliminates the expensive and time-consuming processes of creating and maintaining test records.
- It enables QA teams to use prepackaged test assets and best practices to implement test automation for leading enterprise resource planning (ERP) and customer relationship manager (CRM) applications, which saves time and leverages the knowledge of experts.
- It raises the adoption rate for test automation because it's so easy to deploy and use.

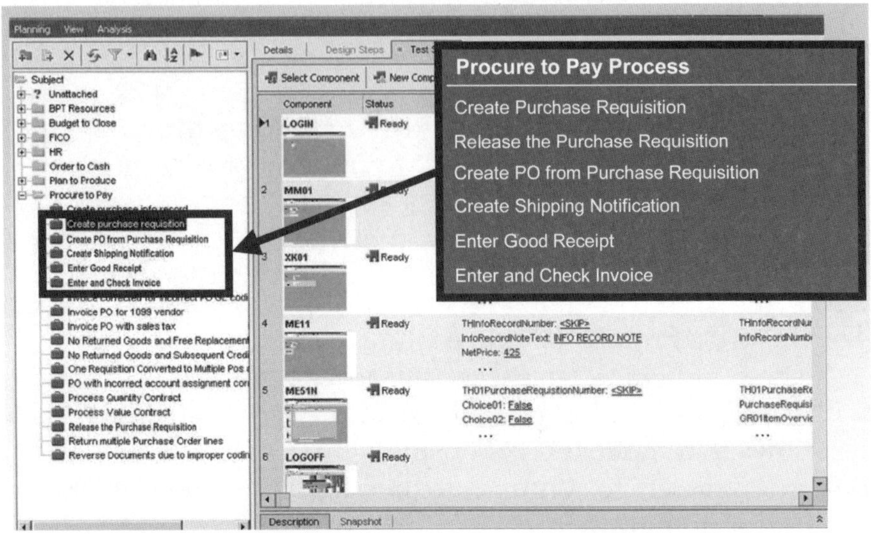

Figure 59: Examples of components and business processes

To demonstrate the advantages of business process testing, let's look at the flight-booking application from Chapter 2. In that case, the process that needs to be tested would look like Figure 60.

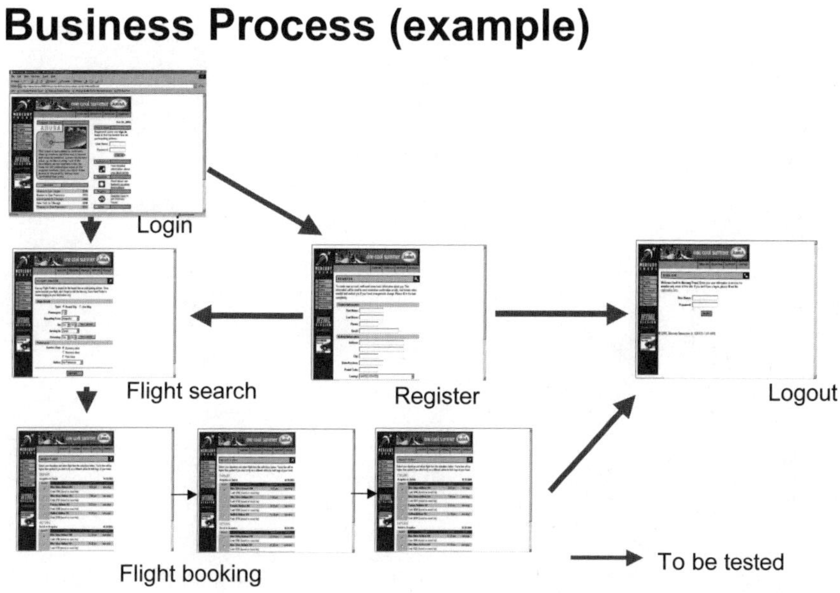

Figure 60: Sample business process for a flight application

Let's now assume that a small change in the LOG IN business function introduces two new fields, because we'll integrate a new business process (Figure 61).

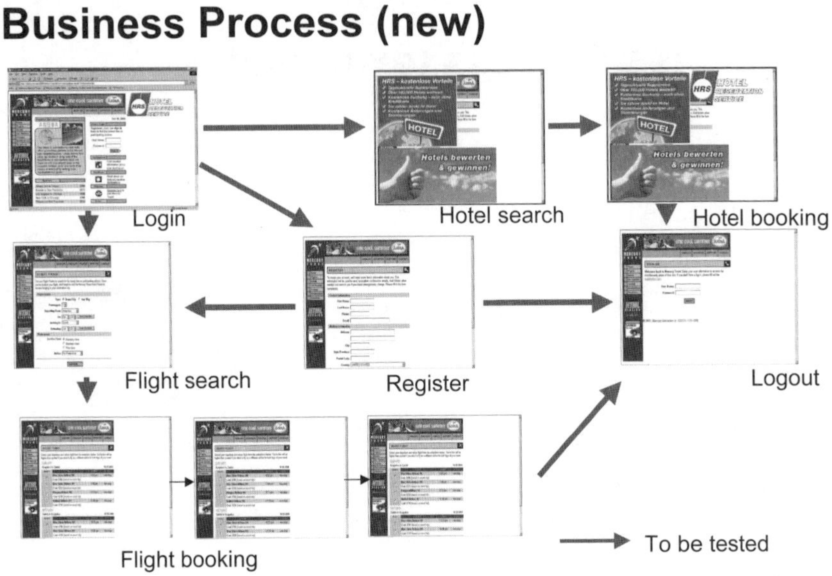

Figure 61: Sample flight application with new business process

In the old days, all the scripts using LOG IN would have to be adapted, which is a major rework effort. With BPT, the change only has to take place in one component and after that, the whole automation works again.

Hence BPT lays the foundation for successful test automation with increased efficiencies and acceptable maintenance effort.

In an ideal world, we could generate the test automation based on the specification, or better yet, the requirement. But, in the real world, we always recommend that you run the test at least once manually before you automate to verify that the test case properly covers the requirements.

The advantage of using BPT is that it is a framework that works for both manual and automated testing. It allows us to design test components as early as the requirements-definition phase, before the business function is fully programmed or developed.

This means we can start testing much earlier, but it also means that we can now align the design of the test components much more closely with the business requirements.

Also, we no longer have to follow the old two-step process of creating manual test cases — verify them once and then create automated tests. With BPT, this is a one-step process (Figure 62).

> Using the business-process testing framework to enhance the traditional test automation technologies and concepts allows us to achieve a better software quality level with the same quality investment.

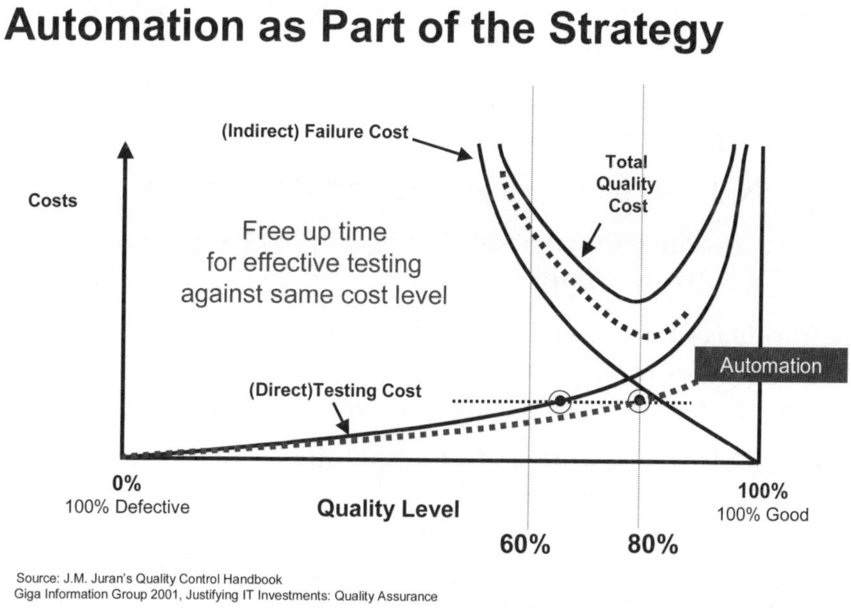

Figure 62: Automation and test frameworks allow higher quality level at a lower total cost

Improving Regression Test Efficiency

Although many organizations now pay more attention to quality process and testing efficiencies for new applications or projects, testing processes for patches, minor releases, and upgrades are generally poor. There are several reasons for this.

Most new implementations involve a large staff, with a budget for enough time and resources. After an application goes live, only a small team of developers and testers are kept to maintain the system. Given that almost every change to a production system is deemed critical, the already reduced testing team never has enough time to run through the proper regression tests.

The increased complexity of today's applications only adds to the problem — every patch to a system possibly impacts dozens of others.

Test planning becomes a very difficult task. Testing teams faced with these challenges can:

- Ask for enough time to run through a full 100 percent regression to ensure all bases are covered.
- Test only the changed component and hope it has no impact on other areas of the application.
- Not test changes at all and cross their fingers.
- Convince management to reject the changes (which hardly ever happens).

Regardless of what they decide, risk is either significantly increased from not testing enough or effort is wasted if a full 100 percent regression is run for every change.

Change Impact Testing™ (CIT) is gaining a lot of traction. The new technology aims to perform a change-impact analysis for every patch or minor release, and then determine exactly which application modules are impacted and which test cases must be regression tested.

So instead of having to run a full regression, we only need to test a small percentage of the regression tests that cover the impacted modules of the application. This solution assures that we can release applications with the highest quality at the lowest level of risk (Figure 63).

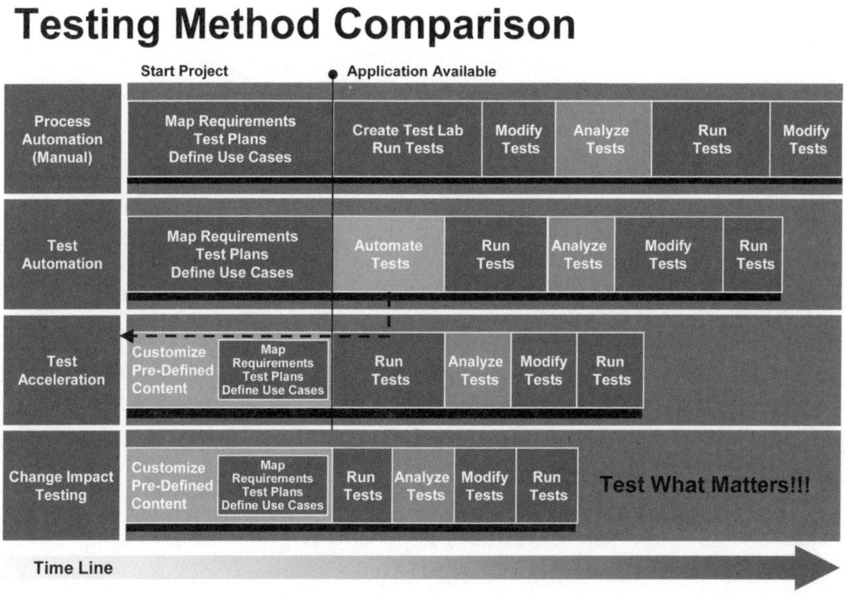

Figure 63: Change Impact Testing can drastically reduce the testing effort

So far in this book, we have discussed testing strategies and concepts that, when leveraged properly, can help drastically improve testing efficiencies and cost effectiveness.

We can implement each separately or together to gain the most benefits. No matter how many techniques you implement or ways you optimize testing, you won't really know if it has improved your software quality unless you can measure, analyze, and compare your testing efforts and software quality over time.

In the next chapter, we discuss our *SUCCESSFUL* goal-driven approach to measuring.

Chapter 6

SUCCESSFUL Goal-Driven KPI Approach

"Count what is countable, measure what is measurable, and what is not measurable, make measurable."
- Galileo, (1564-1642)

In the previous chapters, we've presented a formalized and practical approach to software testing. We want it to be easy to understand, but more importantly, easy to implement.

Many in the industry today still see testing processes as fluff created by business consultants or universities to add overhead and paperwork to already over-burdened staff. Testing processes *can* be very rigorous, and they take dedication and time to prove their value. And busy managers may neglect to measure progress or track test results to determine if the adopted testing process adds enough value for the effort it takes.

Without seeing real successes, many organizations abandon their formalized testing processes.

> Blindly following and implementing testing processes has been the downfall of many quality initiatives.

The good news is that many organizations are implementing quality metrics to give management more visibility into their quality initiatives in order to help them make business decisions.

The biggest challenge to this initiative is determining what to measure and what key performance indicators (KPIs) to use. A KPI is a quantifiable metric applied over a period of time to measure an organization's current status and progress in achieving its business goals.

Because this book aims to align testing with business outcomes, we want to determine if the testing process the business adopts (whether MQM or another) really contributes to the improvement of these business objectives. We also want to see if adopting these testing processes allows organizations to continuously improve on their testing efficiency and effectiveness.

But what do we measure? What KPIs should we use to help us make this determination?

In this chapter, we present a simple goal-driven, top-down approach to determine what to measure and what metrics to use, based on the business objectives and business goals (Figure 64).

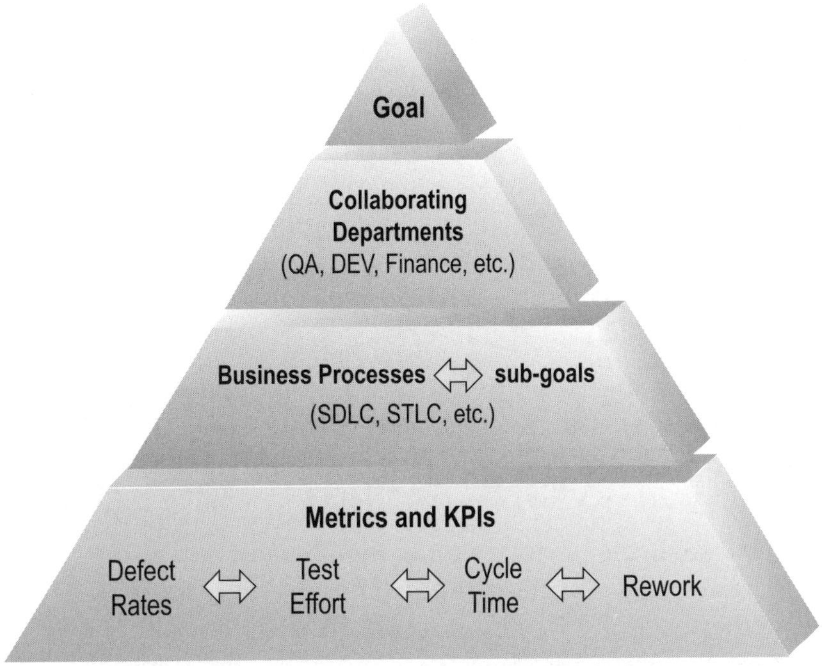

Figure 64: A goal-driven, top-down KPI approach

Business goals should determine what to measure and what KPIs to use. After all, if the KPIs aren't aligned with what the business is set up to achieve, why bother to track those KPIs at all?

Organizations are sometimes confused when tasked with creating a report or dashboard for a specific goal. Everyone has ideas and suggestions of what metrics to use and the conversation often becomes a very technical one. This leads to creating metrics that can't be interpreted or turn out not to be useful in addressing the business questions at hand.

Don't ask, "What types of metrics should I use?" Instead, focus on what you really need to learn or understand about the business.

> One of the axioms of metrics is: What gets measured gets done. So ask, "What do we want done?"

When you fully understand what you need to learn or understand about the business and what factors directly affect the business, figuring out what to measure and what KPIs to use will become more apparent.

Many organizations fail to involve all the departments when they design the metrics. If each department that affects the business goal is not engaged in the process, the measurements can be inaccurate. Why? Because data is probably missing.

Even worse, if the various departments can't agree on measurements, we can't compare the results from those departments, and it becomes more difficult to make sense of what we're measuring because we're no longer comparing apples to apples.

Here are a few items that should be considered in setting up KPIs:

- The technical staff needs to be involved to determine the best ways to gather and process the data that make up the KPIs.
- A normalization and collaboration process has to take place so all departments agree on the KPIs and use the same language and definition for the values of the KPIs.
- Think about what to do after you have obtained the values of the KPIs. Having KPIs and values without an action plan to execute on them is like knowing all the scores of every sporting event in the future and not having a plan to make a bet.

Okay, now we reveal why we shouted *SUCCESSFUL* at you in the title of this chapter — it spells out the 10 steps of our goal-driven approach to a successful testing endeavor (Figure 65).

These steps come from years of experience and the following formula will set you on the right course for getting the full benefit of your testing efforts:

1. **S**et business goals.
2. **U**nderstand the impact of departments on those business goals.
3. **C**hoose supporting business processes.
4. **C**reate business-process goals.
5. **E**xamine what to measure.
6. **S**tandardize measurements across departments.
7. **S**cope data source and integration needs.
8. **F**ormalize indicators and thresholds.
9. **U**tilize and execute appropriate action plans.
10. **L**ay the groundwork and baseline.

This is an iterative process. Revisit these steps regularly — business goals may change. Or you may discover that the metrics you've chosen are not delivering exactly what you wanted.

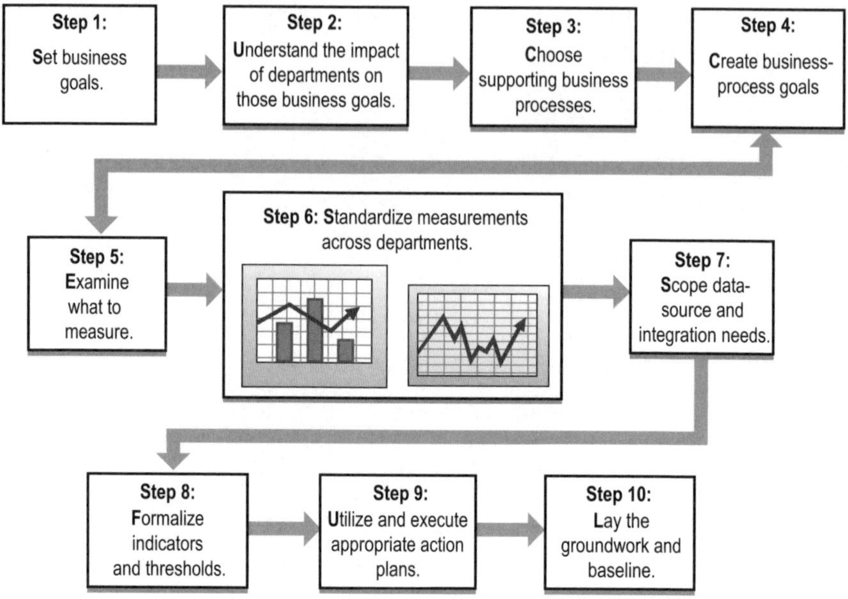

Figure 65: The 10 SUCCESSFUL steps

Set business goals

The first step in our approach should be fairly self explanatory. One can argue that you can never achieve anything without setting goals, because you wouldn't know when you have achieved them. This approach is predicated on setting appropriate business goals.

The purpose of understanding KPIs and creating dashboards and reports to give visibility is to help us make better decisions toward satisfying our business goals.

> Business goals are high-level goals that affect an entire organization or company.

Every organization has such goals — cutting the cost of running the business or getting products to market faster.

Every individual in the organization or company is striving toward these goals.

It's important to note that we use the term business *goals* and not business *objectives*. These terms are often used interchangeably in the industry.

From our perspective, business objectives are determined first — the need to cut IT cost, the need to improve customer service, etc.

Business goals are typically derived from those business objectives, but the key difference is that we can quantify the goals — they have to be measurable. For example, a business goal is to cut IT costs by 20 percent. Or, we have to improve customer satisfaction ratings on a scale of 1–10 by two points.

> How can you determine if you've achieved your business *objectives* without some way to quantify whether you're reaching your business *goals*?

Typically, these business goals are set by the heads of the organizations with input from their direct reports so the goals are reachable.

The number of high-level business goals is typically few — around three or so — as most organizational heads want resources to be targeted in key areas. Having too many goals at one time can only add confusion and make each individual goal difficult to achieve.

It's helpful to ask questions around the business goals to better understand them — the answers will be useful later when determining indicator thresholds. Ask what the internal goals are, versus external goals. Perhaps the sales target internally is $2 million dollars, while the target set externally is only $1.8 million dollars.

Many organizations set a higher internal goal than their external goal, so even a slight shortfall of the internal goal will still allow them to make their external goals — making their stakeholders or investors happy.

Also ask questions that help you determine milestones or checkpoints so if progress falls behind, your teams can agree on action plans to catch up. Or in some cases, reality checks may lead you to redefine success in order to make the business goal more achievable.

Understand the impact of each department on business goals

Okay, after business goals have been set and we've investigated the goals thoroughly, we need to focus on the departments that should collaborate on achieving the goals.

> Identify which departments have direct and indirect impacts on a particular goal and you'll make the best business decisions.

Using the business goal of cutting IT costs by 20 percent, we consider various IT departments that could contribute to that cost cutting. Departments that directly impact this goal may include the development team, the QA team, the operations team, the support team, and off-shore teams. Reallocating the resources and budgets of these teams can have a direct effect in the cost of IT.

Indirectly, we may want to consider the demand non-IT departments are putting on the IT teams. For example, a line of business may want to offer an additional service to its customers immediately; however, the internal IT cost of providing this service is astronomical. By re-evaluating this idea, and perhaps outsourcing the implementation of the service to a business partner or delaying the implementation, we can indirectly reduce the pressure put on the IT organization and thereby reduce IT costs (Figure 66).

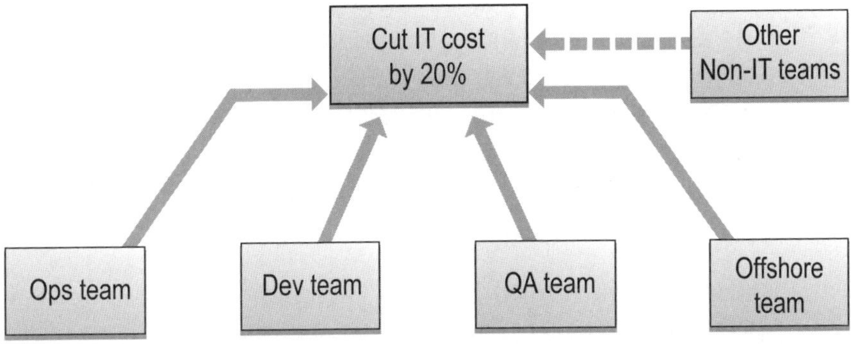

Figure 66: Sample departments that might impact the cost-cutting goal

Choose supporting business processes

Now, for each department that has direct or indirect impacts on the business goal, we must isolate the business processes that could contribute to the business goal. To cut IT costs, we may want to look at the SDLC of the development team to discover if changes can make the SDLC more efficient. In the QA team, we might see if we can improve the effectiveness of the testing process or make the defect process more efficient.

> Evaluate the various attributes of each business process that affects IT costs, such as staff, software, hardware, training, and so on.

By starting with the business processes, we'll see where to streamline those processes before examining the business model attributes in order to determine the action that allows us to best achieve the business goal.

> This approach allows us to take a step back and strategize at a higher level and consider the overall business model before making tactical decisions.

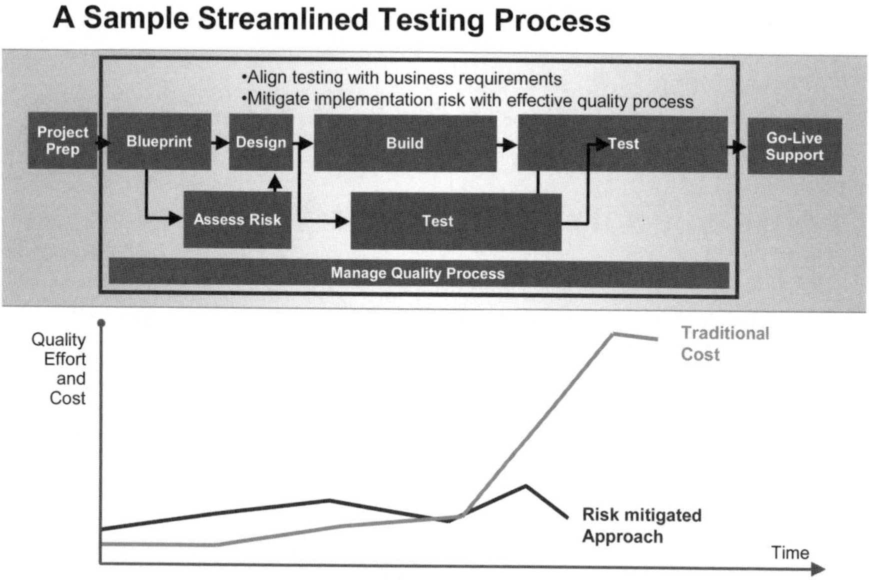

Figure 67: A sample risk mitigated-testing process that may help cut IT costs

Create business process goals

Business process goals are subgoals derived from the business processes described in the last section. They should also align with the business goal.

The logic is that setting cost-cutting goals for a business process within the departments and aligning them with the original business goal of cutting IT costs by 20%, we can be confident that the business process goals are also aligned with the business goals.

> Limit these goals to just a few so you get a clear picture of what you're trying to learn and they're not too hard to track or interpret.

Let's continue with the example of trying to cut IT costs by 20 percent. Using the testing process from the QA team, we can derive a simple process goal to cut the total testing cost by 20 percent.

We can also create subgoals of this process goal. One might be to increase test efficiency by 20 percent. Another subgoal could be to create a strategy to determine if outsourcing can help lower testing resource costs by 20 percent.

Examine what to measure

Keep three things in mind when you examine what to measure. The first is a quote from Albert Einstein, one of the smartest people we know of.

1. "Everything that can be counted does not necessarily count; everything that counts cannot necessarily be counted." - *Albert Einstein*

There will always be intangible elements that cannot be counted. And we can count some items that are not aligned with the business goal, but they're probably not important to us. That brings us to the second point.

2. Continue to ask why we measure, and take the accuracy of what you are measuring seriously.

Because we're aligning with business goals and these business goals are what all individuals within an organization are striving for, simply remember that what gets measured gets done. Work done that is not measured often leads to rework or redundancies.

3. Start with a list of quantifiable questions to ask for each subgoal.

We find it's much easier to figure out what metrics to use or what to measure when we ask the right questions — of the right people.

Interviewing those responsible for the subgoals within a department is a good tactic. Also, talk to the people who are familiar with the relevant business process. Ask questions related to the attributes of the business process subgoal.

If our subgoal is to determine a strategy for outsourcing that can lower testing resource costs, we might consider asking questions such as:

- What is the cost ratio between outsourcers and internal resources?
- What is the productivity level of the outsourcers?
- To cut testing costs by 20 percent, how much should we outsource in order to keep the same level of overall productivity?

Based on the answer to these questions, we might then create a strategy to determine how much we can afford to outsource by weighting factors of business/management viability ratings, productivity, and overall internal satisfaction with outsourcers.

We then calculate each of these high-level metrics and support them through a predetermined formula by a set of lower-level metrics. A way to look at productivity is to simply compare the productivity of outsourcers to internal employees, and then correlate that to the cost ratio to determine the ROI of outsourcing.

For example, for the testing-resource outsourcing-productivity metric, the lower-level metrics in Table 3 could help calculate and support the productivity metric.

Metric	Measurement Description	Standard Value
Rejected defects	Measures the time wasted by Development and QA as a result of false defects to improve the ability of QA engineers to identify and report defects	< 5%
Reopen defects	Measures the effectiveness of the bug-fixing process and QA within this process	< 5%
Defect detection time effectiveness	Measures the speed with which QA detects major defects	>50%
Defect-fix ratio	Measures the percentage of defects found and fixed by Development, out of the total defects found by testers	TBD
Regression defects	Measures the type of work outcome and the type of tasks	TBD
Testing design quantity and production	Checks the type of and the effectiveness of tests (number of defects found by the tests)	TBD

Table 3: Sample set of lower-level metric used to determined outsourced testing productivity

Standardize measurements across departments

Although we determine metrics by using the business process subgoals and aligning them with various departments, it's important to use the same metrics across departments when there are similar subgoals. Many times, departments work in silos and either create different sets of metrics for the same subgoal or use different values to represent the same metric.

In the productivity example above, one QA team may use a set of metrics and values, but another QA team that does some outsourcing may come up with a completely different set of metrics or have different standard values of measurements.

> The problem is not the differences themselves, but interpretation of the results of these metrics.

We could not compare the productivity ratings of the two departments unless they collaborate on a metric-value normalization process that can equate different values from different departments.

In the above example, we may consider using a *defect rejection ratio* instead of the number of *rejected defects* so we can compare this metric from two different QA teams working on two different projects.

In some situations, a more meaningful comparison may be to have one project with 20 *regression defects* and fewer total defects weigh the same as another project with 50 *regression defects* and more total defects.

> The idea is to find ways to interpret data with accuracy and be able to properly compare data across departments.

This step will also help you get agreement between departments on what's important to measure and help teams agree on the metrics and the interpretations of these metrics.

Scope data source and integration needs

At this point, we've determined the metrics and documented them. We've standardized and gained agreement across organizations.

Now we need to determine the data source of the metrics and if any data needs to be integrated to produce the reports and the dashboard views we need for evaluating them.

We might determine that the outsourcing-financial data will come from an ERP system, the testing data will come from Mercury's Quality Center platform, and other IT governance data will come from Mercury's ITG project and portfolio modules.

> Always weigh the feasibility and ease of getting the data when creating metrics and allocate enough resources and time to set up the technology required to capture the data you want.

Formalize indicators and thresholds

Simply having the right metrics and data that map to the goals isn't enough. You must have a set of rules or indicators to help you interpret the data.

The rules used to interpret the data are data thresholds, which should allow you to easily understand the data and to make business decisions.

> Data thresholds must be agreed upon so anyone looking at the data will interpret it the same way.

Using the productivity example again, we might set thresholds at 90 percent and 70 percent. So, if the outsourcer's productivity is 90 percent and above, compared to the internal resources, we determine that to be *great* and associate the number with a green indicator. If the outsourcer's productivity is between 70 and 90 percent, then we consider this a *warning* status and associate the number with a yellow indicator. If the outsourcer's productivity is below 70 percent, we consider this a *failure* and associate it with a red indicator.

These thresholds help us generate the reports and the dashboard views that management can understand (Figure 68).

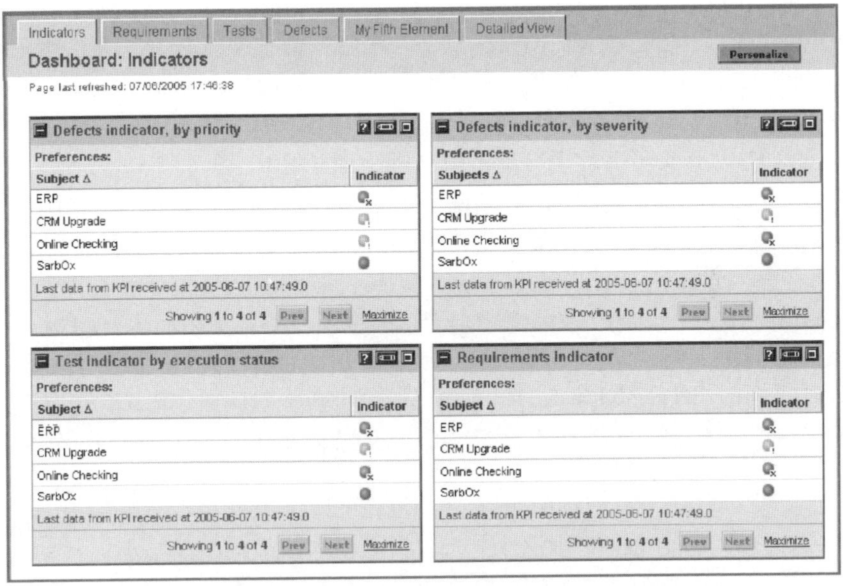

Figure 68: Sample view of a dashboard with indicators

Many people confuse reports and dashboards. Often, dashboard tools are used as reporting tools and vice versa. Let's discuss the differences and reduce the confusion.

> A *dashboard* provides up-to-date dynamic snapshots or indicators of the current state of the business, which allows an individual to make fast business decisions.

> A *report* tells a more detailed story and discusses the process of how the business got to its current state.

A good example of dashboard indicators is what happens when you check stock prices. The vicissitudes of dynamic stock pricing allows you make quick decisions about selling or buying the stock. You may also set thresholds to automatically sell or buy the stock, based on this information.

A report, in this instance, might be the financial report of the same stock that discusses the business conditions for the past year, the detailed process of how the business was run and perhaps the market condition that influenced the price of the stock. This is a more detailed secondary analysis to help you understand the stock, after you determine from the indicator that something is either very good or very bad about the stock.

> Trying to provide every bit of data or metric possible in a dashboard or report creates clutter that makes it difficult to find the data you need to see.

Including too much information makes it harder to implement reporting, and it often causes problems with systems that host the dashboard and/or reports.

Utilize and execute appropriate action plans

All the preparation to determine the KPIs and thresholds aligned with the business goal comes down to the action plans associated with them.

> Be prepared to act, based on the predefined thresholds.

Can you imagine learning all the probabilities and statistics of poker and then not having an action plan to either bid or fold when the appropriate pot odds appear? You would have wasted your effort collecting all that data.

> An action plan is a series of tasks or decisions to follow or make when a certain threshold level is reached.

In Figure 69, we determine that if the outsourcing indicator is green, we should look into outsourcing more in order to cut testing resource costs. If the outsourcing indicator is yellow, we would maintain the status quo. But if the outsourcing indicator is red, we would start to decrease outsourcing and replace outside contractors with more internal resources. Note: in this book, the colors green, yellow, red will show up as gray, white, and black.

Always associate action plans with indicators and be ready to execute your plans immediately to respond to the dynamic changes of today's business environment.

Outsourcer Productivity

Team's Productivity bottom line	July
Integrations	102%
CRM	93%
AR Module	96%
AP Module	94%
Time tracking	82%
Billing	79%
Regression	60%
In-source team	100%

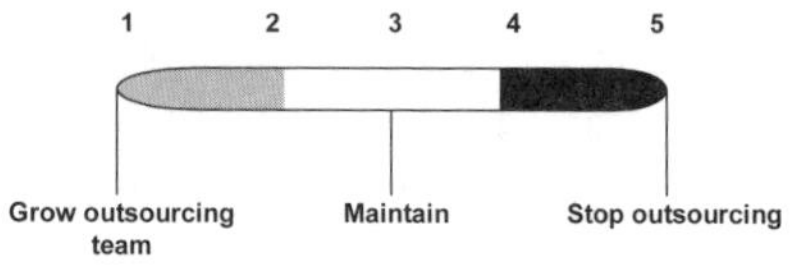

Figure 69: Sample outsourcing indicator with actions

Lay the groundwork and baseline

Remember we mentioned continuous improvement earlier? The only way to see that continuous improvement is to have a good understanding of the initial state of the business, and periodically compare the original state to the current state.

> Take a snapshot of the initial state of the business and use this data as the baseline of comparison during a time in the future.

The first nine steps of this approach have helped us determine all the items we need for the implementation. In this final step, we simply implement the KPIs through standard reports and dashboards, then we compare the snapshots of the business now with where we started.

In summary, the *SUCCESSFUL* goal-driven KPI approach is a logical and simple series of steps to follow to create a measurement strategy.

The 10-step process we've outlined is an iterative process — every time a business goal is reached, we need to revisit these

10 steps to set new goals and determine which items to modify to realign with the new business goals.

We have now introduced our entire software testing approach based on our experiences and the Mercury Quality Model. In the next chapter, we bring the concepts of this book together and help you understand how to start implementing our practical approach to software testing.

Chapter 7

Getting Started: Putting It All Together

We have discussed many things so far, and now it's time to put them all together in a way that will help you with your projects. Let's consider two different situations.

The first occurs at the beginning of a project when you're planning how you'll create, test, and deploy some new application or changes to an existing application. The second situation is, unfortunately, more common: you're in the middle of the test, things are not going as planned, and the deadline is looming. Now what?

Because you're probably in the second situation (and that's probably why you're reading this book), let's talk about that one. Instead of doing everything we've talked about so far, you only have time for a subset, so what should you do?

1. **Structure the application from a business point of view.** Divide it into main processes, subprocesses, and business functions, and link the requirements with the business functions.
2. **Prioritize the business functions.** In the time you have left, concentrate on the important things. You probably won't have time to test all the requirements, so this

involves decisions to withdraw or deploy requirements. These are risk decisions, and the answers will be different for different requirements.

Earlier testing may have already addressed some of these requirements, and that information will be useful in your decisions. (It's important to inform the business stakeholders at this point which requirements you're not going to test.)

3. **Create behavioral models for high-priority business functions only.** You probably don't have time to go back and model the entire application, so focus on the most important requirements.
4. **Link all test cases to the requirements.** Do this for the new test cases you create based on the behavioral models, as well as for all the existing test cases you're running or plan to run.

   The reasons for doing this are twofold. It allows us to make sure we're testing the high-priority business functions. It also reduces the number of test cases that may be necessary to complete the remaining schedule, and you don't want to drop any test cases that are actually helping to meet the objectives. If you can't link a test case to a requirement, consider dropping that test case.
5. **Link any defects found to test cases and requirements.** When everything is connected to everything in this way, we increase visibility and therefore improve project management.
6. **Report on requirement status.** Just as when you link defects to requirements, this type of reporting increases visibility and improves project management.
7. **Leverage prebuilt testing assets.** Finally, if you are in the middle of creating test cases or perhaps attempting to automate enterprise resource planning (ERP) applications, you can leverage some significant prebuilt

testing assets and increase your testing efficiency by up to 300 percent from manual testing.

Now let's examine the situation where you have a bit more time for an in-depth approach. In other words, while the preceding situation tells you what to do when you're *heading* for trouble, here we'll assume you have the time to prevent trouble.

To be successful in your quality initiatives, consider all the elements of what we call the "quality ecosystem." These elements have to do with the governance and the testing itself:

- Requirements
- Reporting
- Defect management
- Performance-issue management
- Shared services
- Test environment
- Test planning and design
- KPIs
- Unit testing
- Integration testing
- System testing
- Performance testing
- User acceptance test
- Operational readiness

You may want to modify this list to match the terminology in your organization. There are many ways of referring to these quality elements, especially when it comes to naming the various stages of the software testing life cycle (STLC).

The first step is to figure out what changes you need to make. Then determine where you are today. This will establish a baseline against which you can measure progress. We use the

Mercury Quality Continuum (MQC) to help determine the current state of an organization.

As a guide to quality and process improvement, the MQC defines quality-related characteristics on a progressive scale. The purpose of the MQC is to provide a scale for the baseline of an organization's status — how does it line up with the elements of the quality ecosystem? Locating an organization along the MQC is the first step in determining where to make investments in quality improvement.

The scale is divided into five levels from Level 0 (quality agnostic) through Level 4 (quality expert).

Level 0: Quality Agnostic

The quality agnostic organization is one in which quality is not considered in any processes. There is little or no recognition of the opportunities available or the cost associated with the lack of quality in the products or processes.

This does not mean that Level 0 companies cannot produce articles of value; many software organizations start off this way and mature as time goes by.

> Level 0 organizations are typically quite small with a close-knit staff in constant communication with each other.

Level 1: Quality Initializing

A quality initializing organization often conducts all quality activities and processes with its development and IT personnel who wear multiple hats.

A Level 1 group also performs tests to verify and validate the development, integration, configuration, design, and architecture infrastructure. Although this level generally has no formal QA processes to follow, it's important to recognize that Level 1 organizations can typically point to case studies or independent instances within the organization that indicate a higher level of maturity.

While some groups within a Level 1 organization may follow processes or possess technology that may be arguably more aligned with a higher level, the ranking is based on the propagation of these advantages so they achieve enterprise-wide efficiency and effectiveness. In cases with conflicting rationale (while most departments are more aligned with a Level 1, some departments are really at Level 2), this can guide the progression to Level 2 using hands-on examples within the same organization.

> Level 1 organizations are typically medium to large in size and are reactive to quality problems.

They often rely on individual expertise rather than repeatable process. These companies have recognized the drawbacks of this ad-hoc approach and they're developing process improvements and introducing software products to automate their improved processes. They're also exploring organizational changes to improve quality.

Process characteristics:

- They do not outline or document the requirements-gathering process.
- They send requirements directly to the project manager.
- The organization has no formal review process — they do not review formal requirements or testing.
- Test plans do not cover all the test types.
- They do not evaluate dependencies and business risks.

- The performance optimization process is ad-hoc and sporadic across projects and applications.
- Little or no performance reporting takes place.
- No functional- or component-testing guidelines exist.
- No defect-tracking process for the project takes place.
- They do not track or report standards metrics.

Product characteristics:

- Software support products such as automated testing, version control, and demand management are either not in use or are used only in pockets in the organization.
- There is no shared repository or otherwise common location for the information and documentation relevant to the projects in the organization.

People characteristics:

- Development leads write the majority of planning documents without consulting much with other teams.
- No dedicated quality-focused team exists.
- Developers create tests and are responsible for test-scenario execution.
- Project managers or development leads write test plans.

Level 2: Quality Conscious

The quality conscious organization is "personnel focused" — it relies heavily on individuals and personnel performance. Less weight is given to the technology or process because the quality conscious personnel are isolated from each other and little technology or process exists to help them collaborate.

At this level of the quality maturity scale, we'll likely find that personnel are pushed to their limits to compensate for the lack of technology or processes.

Level 2 organizations are professionally structured for quality assurance, in that quality — as a concept — is known, understood, and pursued by the enterprise. The organization recognizes the intrinsic value (ROI, economies of scale) that quality mechanisms provide to the enterprise's business processes, and so it's beginning to establish a quality ecosystem.

At this stage, the quality ecosystem is mostly project-focused technologies and fundamental project processes, such as requirements-gathering and broad validation techniques. The quality ecosystem includes dedicated personnel (usually technical quality engineers) who deploy quality assurance practices. Project plans include testing activities, and test assets are documented and maintained in some form of repository.

A project QA team conducts testing and is responsible for enforcing quality processes and performance optimization, but no standard has been established. A defect-tracking process is implemented, although it's not part of a larger test-management software platform. Administrative efficiencies that can be realized through technologies are starting to become important, although the ecosystem has no processes to govern these tools.

The ecosystem is split and not cohesive on an enterprise scale, although pockets of efficiencies throughout the lines of businesses point to the possibility of shared technical services as the next logical step. Sharing personnel skill-set efficiencies, workflows, and technical assets from one line of business to another will be the driving force toward a move to Level 3, where the technology helps realize efficiencies.

> Level 2 organizations are typically medium to large companies that are highly federated, made up of disparate organizations or lines of business.

Process characteristics:

- The organization has not outlined nor documented a requirements-gathering process on a consistent basis. Requirements are sent directly by business (or by a higher-level business process, such as "Sizing") to a project manager.
- Project managers or development leads write test plans, but they do not cover all the performance test types.
- The development lead writes the majority of planning documents without consulting much with other teams.
- Dependencies and business risks are not evaluated.
- Performance and functional testing activity processes are ad-hoc and sporadic across projects and applications.
- The organization undertakes little or no performance testing. Performance metrics, reports, diagnostics, and environmental monitoring offer little value even when they are reported. Any performance-testing processes included in this phase are not necessarily in synch with functional testing.
- A formal quality process for all testing projects is established and in use. The process is project-based and is intended for short-term project-focused initiatives. (No portfolio initiatives exist organically within the quality ecosystem — the many project initiatives are disconnected from each other, but together serve the portfolio's objectives.)
- A quality-review process is in place. Artifacts for the review are produced in a basic format and template. The review process focuses on technical specifications only, not business requirements.
- Defect tracking is taking place, although visibility is limited to the project level — not across all projects and visibility is not offered upstream to management.

- Change-management processes are systematic and follow a known procedure, although not necessarily the same across each project. Control for the change-approval process is dispersed.

Product characteristics:

- Project-level, demand-management software is not in place that links to quality-assurance software, although manual processes exist to facilitate the movement of demand from request to test. For example, data-acquisition demand processes are manual by way of email or phone.
- Version-control tools are leveraged for both documentation management and technical-asset management to some extent.
- A shared repository is in place for storage of various types of business and technical assets. However, no linkage exists between these two types — the repository is not capable of doing this.
- Basic automation has been introduced to the QA team and is implemented where possible. Complex tasks are not automated. Some tasks are left for manual operation, usually because of limited resources (budget limitations and lack of time needed to learn about the automation strategy or train for product adoption) and the lack of implementation experience.
- Efforts to integrate disparate software mechanisms for QA reporting, automation, and management needs are highly unreliable. Reporting software is not standardized across the enterprise, although some standard metrics have been identified.
- If any monitoring of the systems under test is taking place, it is manual.
- One or more reporting tools are in place. They convey status, but there is little integration with the quality-

assurance software that produces the information. Linkage is manual at best, and logical correlation between the various reports is difficult or not possible.

- Change-management products do not exist or are not integrated with quality-assurance products. A consolidated and integrated approach is necessary to link the two domains and to facilitate the intended processes for work requests and shared services.

People characteristics:

- A QA role has been formally designated. In many cases, however, the QA person has additional non-QA responsibilities, probably because of budget, and so is under some time pressures. Also many of these teams are not aware of the advantages of automation or test design, and so designating personnel to focus solely on quality assurance does not make sense to them.
- Personnel that complement work streams for QA (business analysts and technical administrators) have been formally designated to support this early stage of the quality ecosystem. There is a commitment to improve communication between business and technology with an effective layer of CRMs.
- A team leader or project manager conducts informal review processes. Reviews are internal only, and oftentimes are ad-hoc. Review processes seem to be more ideally structured and implemented in the CRM category.
- Support personnel are in place, but they usually take a delegation role. The team leader or project manager often plays this role at this level of maturity.
- Some QA personnel are formally trained on QA automation products in use; however, often no follow-up mentoring or hands-on consulting is available after training to complement the new knowledge. (This situation, combined with the lack of opportunity for the

formal QA team to add value to projects, lengthens the adoption and optimization of automation technologies substantially.)

- No process training happens at this level — the processes are left to the users to learn separately.
- Requirements are created by business-level personnel and handed off to QA. The QA team has no feedback mechanism or influence on requirements.

Level 3: Quality Savvy

A company or organization is at the quality-savvy level if they have a dedicated team of QA personnel with expertise in implementation, configuration, maintenance, and support of quality test and monitoring products. This organization should have established official request-management processes to support the various organizational test teams.

A set of product best practices can be replicated consistently across several lines of business and test groups. The quality group acts as the central point of contact and support for all test and monitoring products. They assist and guide test teams in proper performance and product use and in validating the development, integration, configuration, and infrastructure builds per the design specifications.

Standardized data-gathering and reporting processes use automated test and monitoring product solutions.

> Level 3 organizations are typically large, integrated companies with shared infrastructure and common processes. They are often financial, insurance, or medical institutions.

Process characteristics:

- The organization has standard data-gathering and reporting processes.
- Best practices for software test and software development life cycles have been documented.
- Automation guidelines and test-process best practices exist.
- QA uses known standards and collaborative workflows.
- Customer support for products is available.
- Charge back is based on centralized licenses, infrastructure, resources, and product-related service requests.
- Business-case and ROI analysis for products is in place.
- Demand-management processes are in place.
- Cross-project test management and performance-test reporting are in place.
- A center of excellence exists, with a shared, consulting-services framework and funding/charge-back options.
- The company has internal billing capabilities.
- A test lab infrastructure is operational.
- The organization implements risk mitigation, has established quality gates, and applies exit criteria before moving into the next phase of the SDLC.
- Service-level reporting is in place.
- Business-case templates and procedures have been developed.
- An internal marketing process exists for services shared across business units.
- A formal communication process is established between all teams.

- Testing services are provided across multiple lines of business.

Product characteristics:

- Automated testing is in use throughout the organization.
- Product and test lab/infrastructure administration processes are in place.
- Demand management is enforced by ITG product implementation.
- Standard data-gathering and reporting processes use automated test and application-monitoring product solutions.
- Automated test management and performance design is in place.
- A dashboard is implemented with real-time reporting capabilities and test metrics.
- Testing products test application components, business processes, and scenarios.
- A dashboard gives visibility into project status.
- Dashboard validation and certification services are performed.

People characteristics:

- Management focuses on hiring experienced quality-focused technical personnel.
- Experts in test-management, performance-testing, and application-monitoring products are in place.
- Resources are scheduled for product customization, maintenance, and support.
- Training and certification is readily available for staff.
- QA has its own budget.

- QA is involved up front in the SDLC.
- QA estimates the number of hours it needs to complete a testing task and quality work.
- 24/7, enterprise-wide, testing-product infrastructure and support is in place.

Level 4: Quality Expert

An organization is at a quality expert level when it has formal quality processes, often enforced and supported by products, and dedicated product and process QA experts that can be leveraged across the organization. It emphasizes a continuous improvement of process best practices, and uses metrics to measure quality.

In addition, responsibilities of the centralized QA group include creation and certification of quality gate processes, training and mentoring of application test teams, and guidance of process and product implementation. Internal marketing practices are in place and service-level reporting is performed. The service utility may also be involved with or completely manage the performance optimization services, which would include infrastructure tuning (application testing, reliability, scalability, and stress tests).

It is usually the case that Level 4 organizations are thought leaders in best practices and methodology. Level 4 organizations typically have personnel with black belts in Six Sigma, and/or follow industry-standard quality procedures such as those found in ITIL.

The monetary cost of entry into the Level 4 domain is high, and it's the main consideration for most organizations. For instance, if the cost of moving from Level 3 to Level 4 is drastically higher than the benefit added to the quality ecosystem, there is understandably little rationale for investing in such an ambition.

> Level 4 organizations are completely driven by quality, and can only exist by employing strict quality standards that meet government-imposed or industry-imposed regulations or restrictions.

Process characteristics:

- A formal communication process is established.
- Quality validation and certification services are performed.
- Metrics have been agreed upon and reporting at the centralized application level is obtained.
- Cross-project test management and performance-test reporting is done.
- Test automation training and mentoring capabilities are in place.
- Known standards and collaborative workflows govern the day-to-day activities of the organization. The organization cannot exist without complete adherence to these standards.

Product characteristics:

- Automated service-level reporting (service level of the utility) is in place.
- An industry-standard quality model is used.
- All quality reviews, quality gates, and process reviews are standardized.
- Standardized services and metrics are based on best practices.
- A dashboard is in place that gives organization-wide visibility into the status of all projects.

- IT governance solutions digitize most quality ecosystem workflows.

People characteristics:

- Advanced test engineering personnel provide testing services across multiple lines of businesses.
- Functional test organization and automation expertise is reviewed by certified industry standards organizations. Functional and/or performance testing is always completed to government or industry specifications.
- Project/test management expertise is typically in line with PMO-based structures such as the PMI.
- Certified industry personnel act as quality managers. Quantified experience and structured certification-based training is mandatory to achieve this level.

Self Evaluation — Designing a Roadmap

When we work with client organizations to help with quality improvement, we first determine their current level, develop a set of recommendations, and design a roadmap for implementing the recommendations. Our process looks like Figure 70.

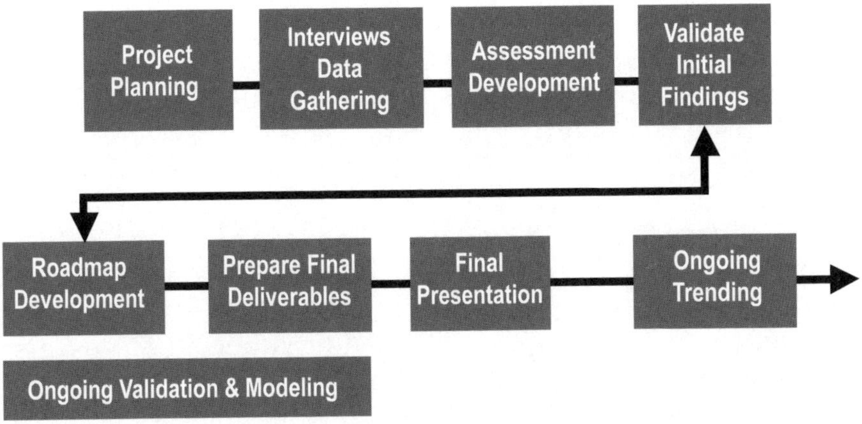

Figure 70: A sample self evaluation and quality planning process

To put this in context for you, most of the organizations we see start off in the mid-Level 1 to mid-Level 2 range.

When you start applying the concepts, practices, and recommendations in this book, it is useful to approach a transition from where you are with two perspectives in mind — strategic and tactical.

The strategic approach is to decide where you want the organization to go. Do you want to be at Level 4? Is Level 2 good enough to serve your business goals? These are business decisions. Any advance in quality is an investment, and you must consider the amount to be invested and your organization's tolerance for change.

After you decide on your target level, it is necessary to determine where you are today. If you're already operating at the level that suits your business goals, declare victory and move on. Most of us, however, have room for improvement.

To determine where you are today, review the quality continuum above. Be very objective in comparing your organization to the descriptions of each level. This comparison will show you areas you can and should improve, and your efforts should focus on those areas.

> Tactically, one of the biggest inhibitors to quality is the all-too-common lack of communication between IT and the business.

More than just getting the requirements agreed upon, business stakeholders and IT need to be in communication throughout the project. IT will want business input for review and test-plan approval. The business will need to understand progress and trends as the IT work continues, so managers can prepare for the changes coming to the software or systems.

This means that establishing a governing body or committee made up of both IT and business stakeholders is very important for the success of any project. The frequency of communication should depend on the risks associated with the project and its current status.

Let's summarize our strategy and tactics.

> Strategy
>
> - Determine where you are and where you want to be.
> - Align quality initiatives to business outcomes.
>
> Tactics
>
> - Build a communication mechanism between IT and business.
> - Implement the changes suggested by your strategic review.

While we are now at the end of the book, this is just the beginning for you. The things we've discussed in this and previous chapters are all a part of what makes a test — and a project — successful. Good luck, and have fun.

Appendix A

Common Test Techniques

In Chapter 1, we described test stages and why they are important. All of the test stages fall into two basic test types, white-box testing and black-box testing. The following lists common test techniques used for each test type.

White-Box Testing Techniques

The seven most common techniques and approaches of white-box testing are described here.

Syntax Testing

ANALYSIS: Syntax testing uses a model of the formally defined syntax of the inputs to a component. We represent the syntax as a number of rules, each of which defines the possible means of production of a symbol in terms of sequences of, iterations of, or selections between other symbols.

DESIGN: We design test cases with valid and invalid syntax from the formally defined syntax of the inputs to the component. Test cases with valid syntax are intended to execute options derived from the following rules (although additional rules may apply):

- Whenever a selection is used, an option is derived for each alternative by replacing the selection with that alternative.
- Whenever an iteration is used, at least two options are derived: one with the minimum number of iterated symbols, and the other with more than the minimum number of repetitions.

A test case may exercise any number of options.

For each test case, specify the following items:

- Input(s) to the component
- Option(s) exercised
- Expected outcome of the test case

Test cases with invalid syntax are designed as follows:

- Document a checklist of generic mutations that can be applied to rules or parts of rules, in order to generate a part of the input that is invalid.
- Apply this checklist to the syntax to identify specific mutations of the valid input, each of which employs at least one generic mutation.
- Design test cases to execute specific mutations.

For each test case, specify the following items:

- Input(s) to the component
- Generic mutation(s) used
- Syntax element(s) to which the mutation or mutations are applied
- Expected outcome of the test case

Statement Testing

ANALYSIS: Statement testing uses a model of the source code that identifies statements as either executable or nonexecutable.

DESIGN: We design test cases to exercise executable statements.

For each test case, specify the following items:

- Input(s) to the component
- Identification of statement(s) the test case should execute
- Outcome you expect of the test case

Branch/Decision Testing

ANALYSIS: Branch testing requires a model of the source code that identifies decisions and decision outcomes. A decision is an executable statement that may transfer control to another statement depending on the logic of the decision statement. Typical decisions are found in loops and selections. Each possible transfer of control is a decision outcome.

DESIGN: We design test cases to exercise decision outcomes.

For each test case, specify the following items:

- Input(s) to the component
- Identification of decision outcome(s) the test case should execute
- Outcome you expect from the test case

Data Flow Testing

ANALYSIS: Data flow testing uses a model of the interactions between parts of a component connected by the flow of data as well as the flow of control.

Assign categories to variable occurrences in the component, where the category identifies the definition or the use of the variable at that point.

Definitions are variable occurrences in which you give a new value to a variable. Uses are variable occurrences in which you do not give a new value to a variable. (You can further distinguish uses as either data definition P-uses or data definition C-uses. Data definition P-uses occur in the predicate portion of a decision statement, such as while ... do, if ... then ... else, etc. Data definition C-uses are all others, including variable occurrences in the right-hand side of an assignment statement, or an output statement.)

Derive the control flow model for the component and identify the location and category of variable occurrences on it.

DESIGN: We design test cases to execute control flow paths between definitions and uses of variables in the component.

For each test case, specify the following items:

- Input(s) to the component
- Locations of relevant variable definition and use pair(s)
- Control flow subpath(s) to be exercised
- Outcome you expect from the test case

Branch Condition Testing

ANALYSIS: Branch condition testing requires a model of the source code that identifies decisions and the individual Boolean operands within the decision conditions. A decision is an executable statement that may transfer control to another statement depending on the logic of the decision statement. A decision condition is a Boolean expression you evaluate in order to determine the outcome of a decision. We find typical decisions in loops and selections.

DESIGN: Design test cases to exercise individual Boolean operand values within decision conditions.

For each test case, specify the following items:

- Input(s) to the component
- Each decision evaluated by the test case, identification of the Boolean operand to be exercised by the test case and its value
- Outcome you expect of the test case

Branch Condition Combination Testing

ANALYSIS: Branch condition combination testing requires a model of the source code that identifies decisions and the individual Boolean operands within the decision conditions. A decision is an executable statement that may transfer control to another statement depending on the logic of the decision statement. A decision condition is a Boolean expression we evaluate to determine the outcome of a decision. We find typical decisions in loops and selections.

DESIGN: We design test cases to exercise combinations of Boolean operand values within decision conditions.

For each test case, specify the following items:

- Input(s) to the component
- For each decision evaluated by the test case, identification of the combination of Boolean operands to be exercised by the test case and their values
- Outcome you expect from the test case

Modified Condition Decision Testing

ANALYSIS: Modified condition decision testing requires a model of the source code that identifies decisions, outcomes, and the individual Boolean operands within the decision conditions. A decision is an executable statement that may transfer control to another statement depending on the logic of the decision statement. A decision condition is a Boolean expression that is evaluated to determine the outcome of a decision. We find typical decisions in loops and selections.

DESIGN: We design test cases to demonstrate that Boolean operands within a decision condition can independently affect the outcome of the decision.

For each test case, specify the following items:

- Input(s) to the component
- For each decision evaluated by the test case, identification of the combination of Boolean operands to be exercised by the test case, their values, and the outcome of the decision
- Outcome you expect from the test case

Black-Box Testing Techniques

The four most common techniques and approaches of black-box testing are described here.

Smoke Test

A subset of the black-box test is the smoke test. This test is a cursory examination of all of the basic components of a software system to ensure that they work. Typically, smoke testing is conducted immediately after a software build is made.

The term comes from electrical engineering, where in order to test electronic equipment, power is applied and the tester ensures that the product does not spark or smoke. This test ensures that future testing is not blocked.

Equivalence Partitioning

ANALYSIS: Equivalence partitioning uses a model of the component that partitions the input and output values of the component. The input and output values are derived from the specification of the component's behavior.

Each partition contains a set or range of values, chosen so that all the values can reasonably be expected to be treated by the component in the same way (that is, they may be considered equivalent). Valid and invalid values are partitioned in this way.

DESIGN: We design test cases to exercise partitions. A test case may exercise any number of partitions and the following items must be specified:

- Input(s) to the component
- Partitions exercised
- Outcome you expect from the test case

Test cases are designed to exercise partitions of valid values and invalid input values. We may also design test cases to check that invalid output values cannot be induced.

Boundary Value Analysis

ANALYSIS: Boundary value analysis uses a model of the component that partitions the input and output values of the component into a number of ordered sets with identifiable boundaries. These input and output values are derived from the specification of the component's behavior.

The model comprises bounded partitions of ordered input and output values. Each partition contains a set or range of values, chosen so we can reasonably expect all the values to be treated by the component in the same way (that is, they may be considered equivalent). Both valid and invalid values are partitioned in this way. We normally define the partition's boundaries by the values of the boundaries between partitions; however, where partitions are disjointed, we use the minimum and maximum values in the range that makes up the partition. We consider the boundaries of both valid and invalid partitions.

DESIGN: We design test cases to exercise values both on and next to the boundaries of the partitions. We produce three test cases for each identified boundary, corresponding to values on the boundary and an incremental distance on either side of it.

We define this incremental distance as the smallest significant value for the data type under consideration.

For each test case, specify the following items:

- Input(s) to the component
- Partition boundaries exercised
- Outcome you expect from the test case

Test cases are designed to exercise valid boundary values and invalid input boundary values. We may also design test cases to test that invalid output boundary values cannot be induced.

User Input Validation

You must validate user input to conform to expected values. For example, if the software program is requesting input on the price of an item and is expecting a value such as 3.99, the software must check to make sure all invalid cases are handled. A user could enter the price as "-1" and achieve results contrary to the design of the program. Other examples of entries that could be entered and cause a failure in the software include: "1.20.35," "abc," "0.000001," and "999999999." These possible test scenarios should be entered for each point of user input.

Other domains, such as text input, need to restrict the length of the characters that can be entered. If a program allocates 30 characters of memory space for a name, and the user enters 50 characters, a buffer overflow condition can occur.

Typically when invalid user input occurs, the program either corrects it automatically or displays a message to the user that their input needs to be corrected before proceeding.

Appendix B

Quality Solutions Introduction and Overview

Because this book was intended to focus more on practical process and methodologies for testing, we did not invest much time to discuss the technology aspects of testing in detail. It is important to note that most of the concepts presented in this book can be implemented, digitized, or automated with Mercury's Quality Solutions. Here is a list of quality solutions from Mercury that can be leveraged with the concepts in this book.

Quality Center

Mercury Quality Center™ provides a complete web-based integrated system for performing quality assurance across a wide range of environments. Its applications support and automate key quality activities, including requirements management, test management, issue tracking, and automated functional and business-process testing.

Quality Center consists of the following components:

Application Delivery Foundation — Quality Center is powered by an enterprise-level J2EE platform that serves as a central repository for all quality assets, houses centralized workflow rules, and facilitates collaboration among all parties involved in the quality process. The application delivery foundation ensures 24/7 availability, scalability, performance, and redundancy of the Quality Center to make sure that it's available to all users at all times, including complex, geographically distributed Centers of Excellence.

TestDirector™ for Quality Center — Requirements Management, Test Plan, Test Lab, and Defect Management offer a seamless, consistent, and repeatable process for all stages of application quality management — from gathering requirements, to planning and scheduling tests, analyzing results, and managing defects and issues. All Quality Center Management applications are web-based, and traceability is provided and enforced across all parts of the application life cycle.

Application Delivery Dashboard™ — All the information collected during the quality process needs to be processed, aggregated, and analyzed to provide solid basis for decision-making. Unlike the traditional "reports," the Dashboard is designed to provide an executive-level view of the entire quality process. The LOB IT manager, director, or project manager can get a clear understanding of what's going on with the process, project, performance, and quality, across multiple IT projects and initiatives, to make informed release decisions. In addition to reporting the high-level status, the Dashboard provides the drill-down capabilities to help determine the root-cause of a particular problem and take corrective measures.

Business Process Testing™ (BPT) — BPT is the new way to approach test automation. Unlike the traditional record-replay tools, BPT gets business analysts who know the most about application functionality and common uses involved in the process of creating automated, reusable, test components. The business analyst can use familiar tools like spreadsheet grids to describe the common business process flow through the application. Using real language, they can describe what's being done on each screen and what the expected results are. After the business process flows have been documented, the automation engineer — who is familiar with powerful automation solutions like QuickTest Professional™ — creates reusable test components and stores them in the QC repository. The business analyst can then drag-and-drop those components to create complete business processes, such as order entry, customer contact management, etc.

Mercury Functional Testing™ — QuickTest Professional and WinRunner®. QuickTest Professional is an advanced automated testing solution for building functional and regression tests. It features the unique keyword view and active screen technology to radically simplify test creation and maintenance. WinRunner is the standard functional testing solution for enterprise IT applications. It offers a powerful tool for capturing, verifying, and replaying the user actions automatically to identify defects and ensure that applications remain reliable.

Mercury Performance Center

Mercury Performance Center™ is an enterprise-class performance testing platform designed to enable both global standardization and the formation of a performance testing center of excellence (COE). This solution enables standardization and centralization of distributed-application performance testing teams with a single web-based solution.

Mercury LoadRunner® — LoadRunner is the industry-standard performance testing solution; it drives load, diagnoses problems, and deploys with no surprise. Using minimal hardware resources, Mercury LoadRunner emulates hundreds or thousands of concurrent users to apply production workloads to virtually any client platform or environment. Mercury LoadRunner stresses an application from end to end — applying consistent, measurable, and repeatable loads — then uses the data to identify scalability issues that would impact real users in production.

Appendix C

Behavioral Model Glossary

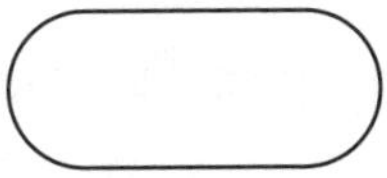

Terminator: start or end

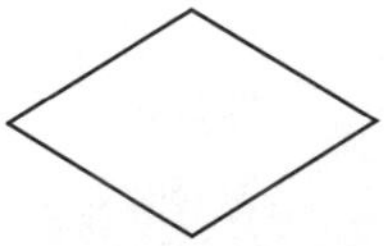

Decision: true or false; yes or no

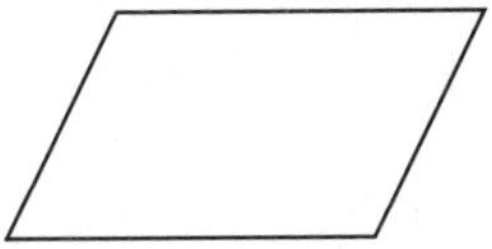

Representative sample

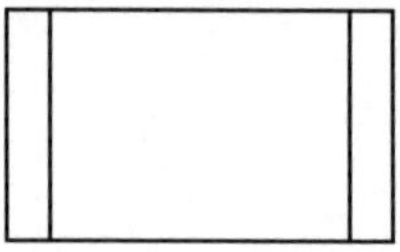

Defined process

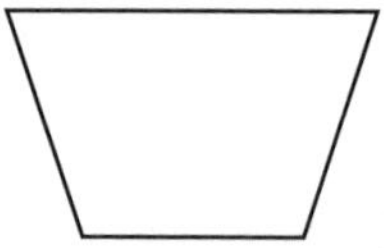

Manual process

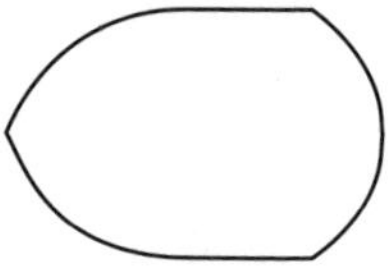

Displayed result (usually an error message)

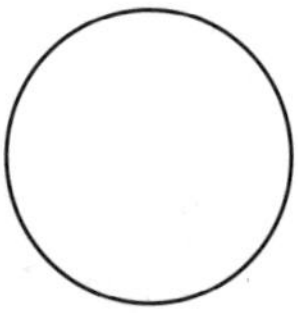

Case

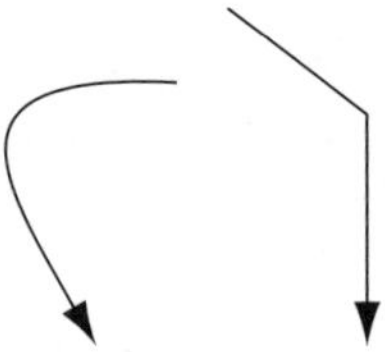

Connectors

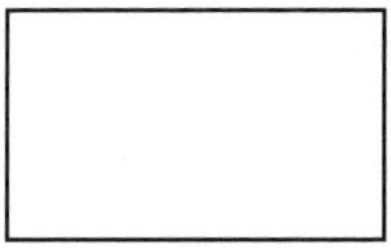

Result

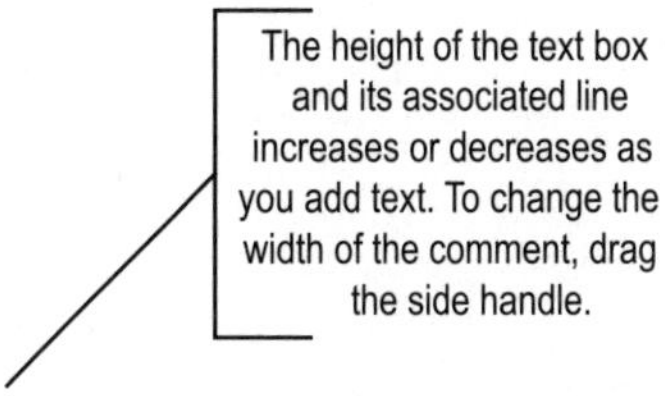
The height of the text box and its associated line increases or decreases as you add text. To change the width of the comment, drag the side handle.

Note

Appendix D

Modeling Tips

As we go through the process of functional decomposition, always look for opportunities to break things down. We are after the simplest representation of the behavior — this results in the least number of tests.

Furthermore, by decomposing into the simplest building blocks, the resultant model is easy to understand. This is a good thing!

Yes, it is possible to break things down too far. Judgment is required here to get the proper balance.

* * *

The "defined process" block shows up in all the levels of the model before the lowest level. Remember that this block should be the only block on the path. Otherwise, we indicate that we want to multiply the number of test cases, not add them.

* * *

Some constructs show up frequently in test design, and there are usually simple ways of handling them. You can create a library for these and just copy-and-paste into your models (making, of course the required editorial changes).

Consider the situation where the software under test has a command line interface. Most often, command line interfaces allow the user to enter several parameters. These parameters must be validated, and, if any of them are incorrect, some action must be taken.

There are two common ways in which the parsing and analysis take place. In the first of these, the software goes through the list, one at a time, checking as it goes. As soon as the software discovers an invalid parameter, it exits and gives an error message. For UNIX programs, this error message is simply a display of the information that describes the usage of the command line.

A slightly more helpful program would issue a message that identifies the specific parameter in error and explains the problem.

Another approach — far more user-friendly — would scan the entire line and give the user information about all the errors at one time rather than requiring the user to reissue the command line as many times as there are erroneous parameters.

The figures on the following pages show how each of these situations is handled in their respective behavior models.

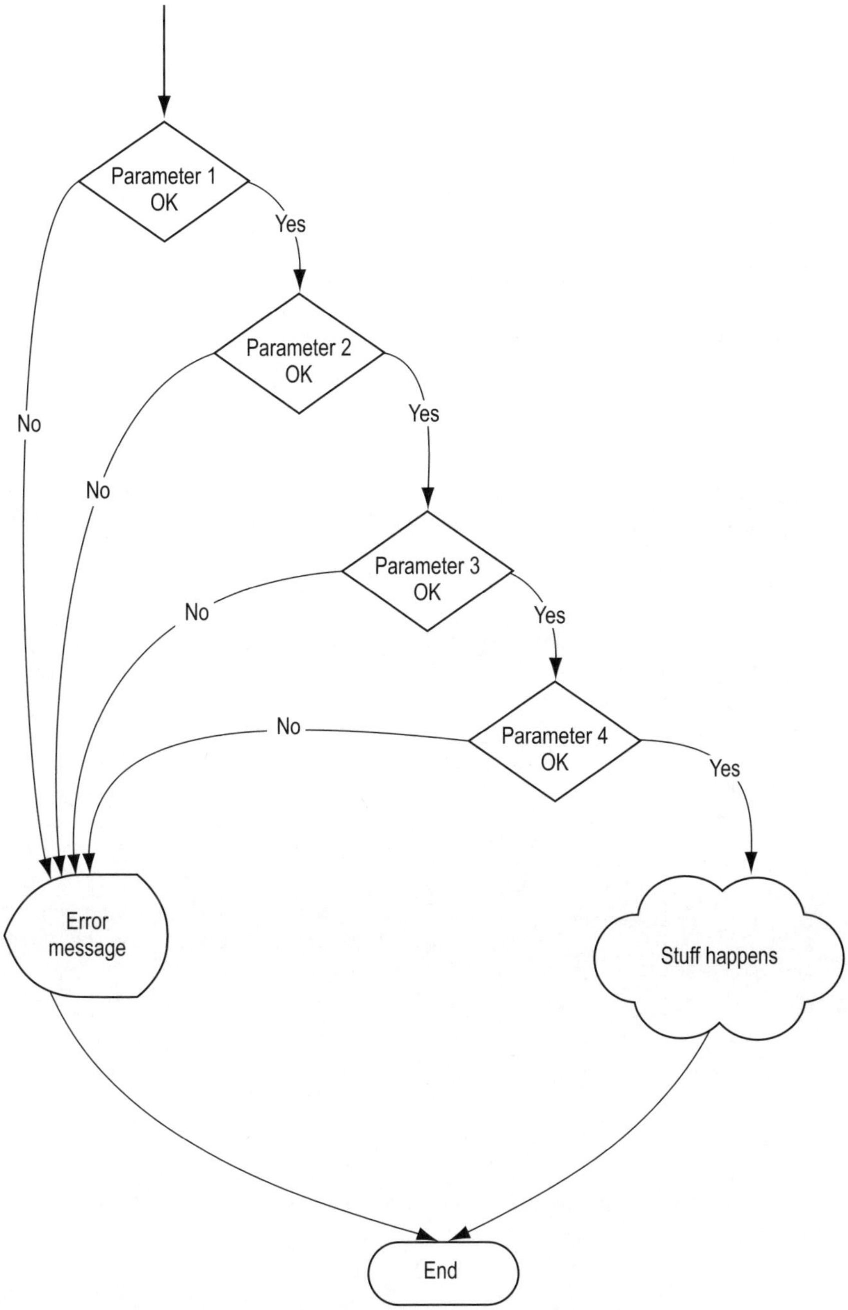

Figure 71: Exit on first error; common error message

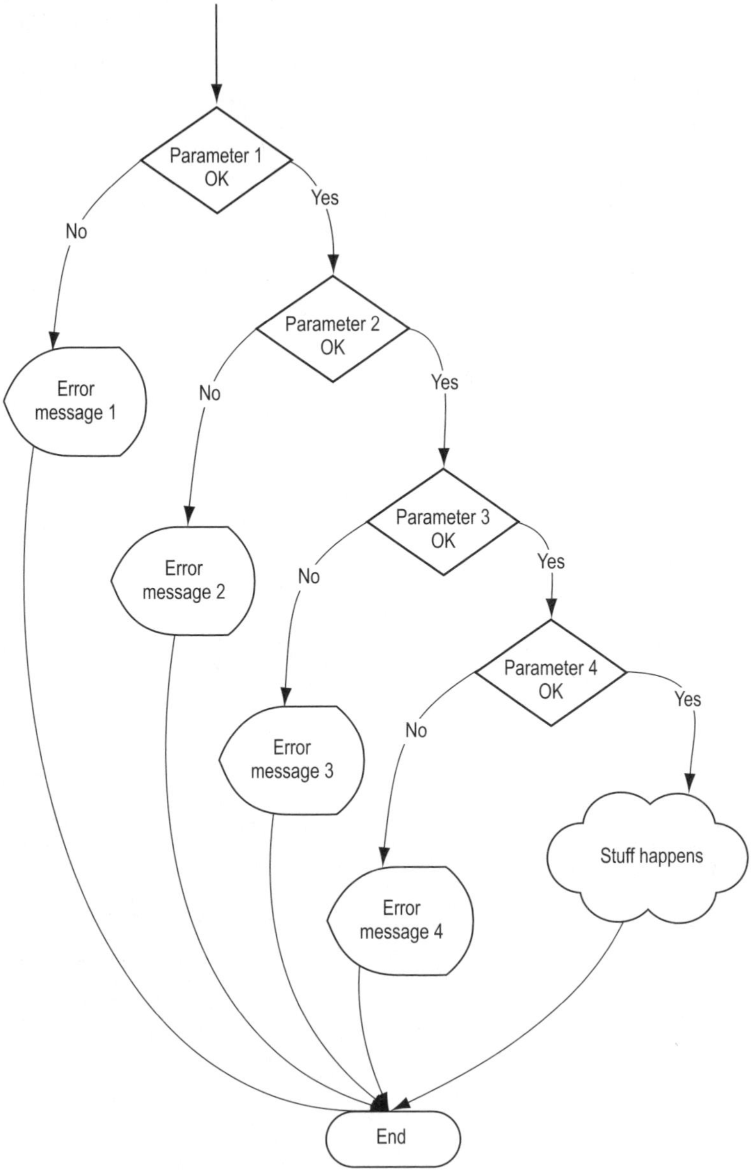

Figure 72: Exit on first error; individual error messages

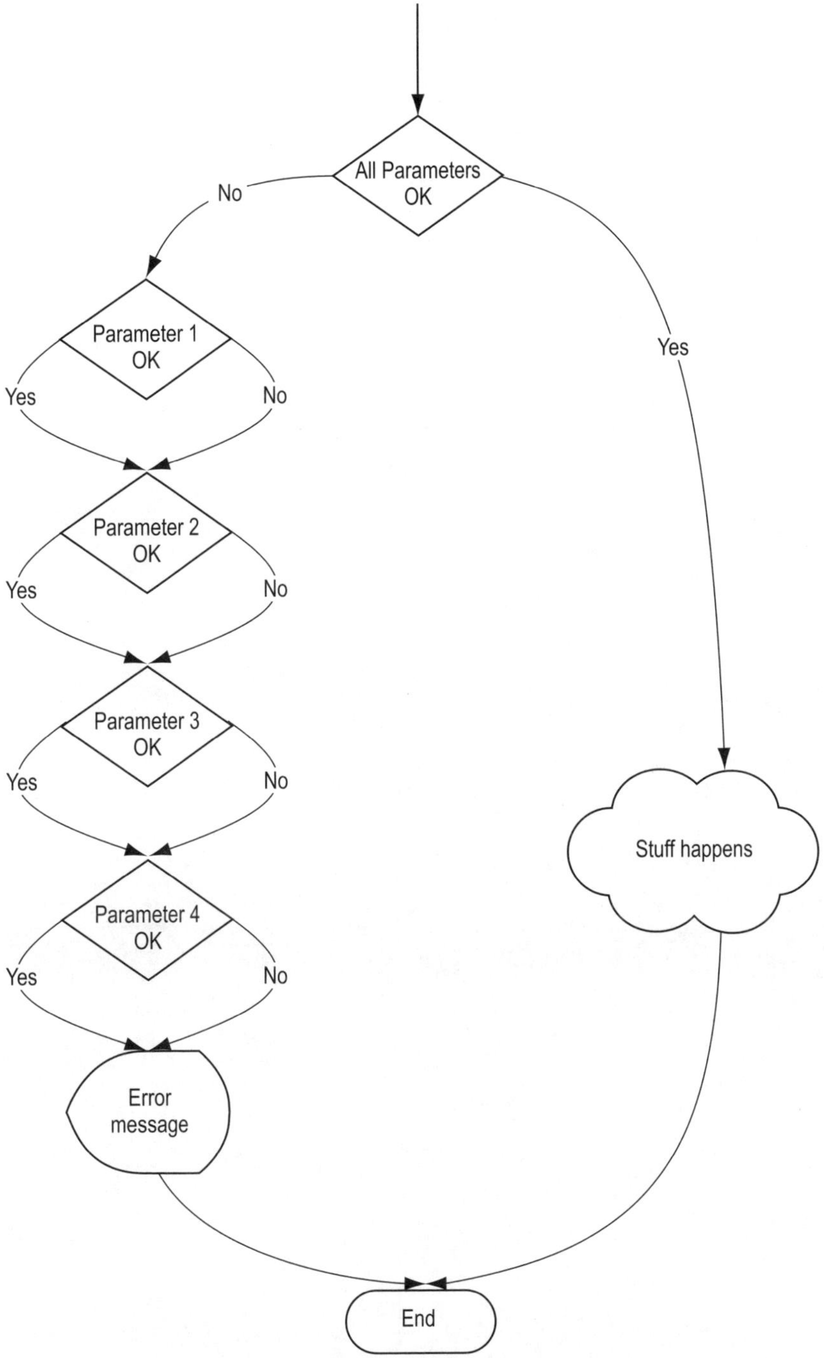

Figure 73: Single-pass scan of input line

Another common situation occurs when the program must handle a multiple choice followed by a multiple choice where these are independent of each other. For example, the program under test must be able to do any of several things, and must do all of these on several operating systems. The model would be a case block followed by another case block.

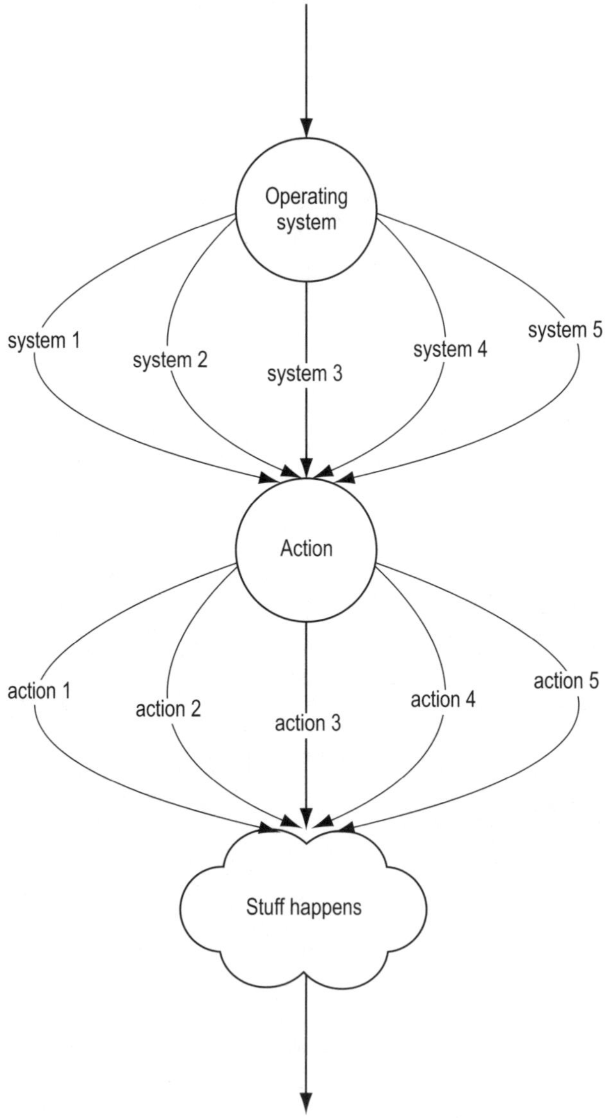

Figure 74: Case after case

Appendix E

FAST Test Case Design

This section contains the entire test case design for FAST. If you have tried to create the FAST TCD on your own, you may want to compare your version with this. Remember, though, that there is rarely one right answer for these, so you may prefer your own version.

TCD ID:	F		
Description:	FAST		
Author:			
Original Release:	1.0	Date:	9/7/20xx

Function:	TCD:	Page:
Balance	FB	
Deposit	FD	
Exceptions	FE	
Sign on	FS	
Transfer	FT	
Withdraw	FW	
String	FR	

Matrix ID: FB								
Description:	FAST Balance							
Author:								
Original Release: 1.0			Date: 9/6/20xx					
Test case:	FB01	FB02	FB03	FB04	FB05	FB06	FB07	FB08
Control Points:								
Account:	*	*	*	*	*	*	*	*
Checking	*		*	*	*			
Savings		*				*	*	*
Account exists?	N	N	Y	Y	Y	Y	Y	Y
Current Balance:			*	*	*	*	*	*
zero			*			*		
non-zero:				*	*		*	*
maximum amount				*			*	
0.01					*			*
Expected Results	"Requested Account Does Not Exist."		Correct balance displayed.					

Matrix ID:	**FD**					
Description:	**FAST Deposit**					
Author:						
Original Release:	**1.0**			**Date: 9/6/20xx**		
Test case:	FD01	FD02	FD03	FD04	FD05	FD06
Control Points:						
To Account:	*	*	*	*	*	*
Checking	*	*	*			
Savings				*	*	*
Account exists?	N	Y	Y	N	Y	Y
Amount of deposit:		*	*		*	*
valid			*			*
invalid		*			*	
Expected Results	"Requested Account Does Not Exist. Re-enter."	"Invalid amount. Re-enter." Re-entered amount accepted.	Account balance updated with the deposited amount.	"Requested Account Does Not Exist. Re-enter."	"Invalid amount. Re-enter."	Account balance updated with the deposited amount.

Matrix ID:	FE					
Description:	FAST Exceptions					
Author:						
Original Release:	1.0		Date: 9/6/20xx			

Test case:	FE01	FE02	FE03	FE04	FE05	FE06	FE07
Control Points:							
Cancel during:	*	*	*	*	*		
balance	*						
deposit		*					
sign-on			*				
transfer				*			
withdraw					*		
Out of paper						*	
FAST out of cash							*
Expected Results	Transaction canceled. Display returns to menu.					"This machine is temporarily out of service."	

Matrix ID: FS			
Description: FAST Sign-on			
Author:			
Original Release: 1.0			**Date: 9/6/20xx**
Test case:	FS01	FS02	FS03
Control Points:			
Valid FAST card:	*	*	*
yes	*	*	
no			*
Account(s) still open:	*	*	
yes	*		
no		*	
Expected Results	User Signed on; main menu displayed	"This card no longer valid." Card retained by FAST	"This is not a FAST card"; card returned.

Matrix ID: FT														
Description: FAST Transfer														
Author:														
Original Release: 1.0			**Date: 9/6/20xx**											
Test case:	FT01	FT02	FT03	FT04	FT05	FT06	FT07	FT08	FT09	FT10	FT07	FT08	FT09	FT10
Control Points:														
To Account:	*	*	*	*	*	*	*	*	*	*	*	*	*	*
Checking	*		*	*	*		*	*	*	*				
Savings		*				*					*	*	*	*
To Account exists?	N	N	Y	Y	Y	Y	Y	Y	Y	Y	Y	Y	Y	Y
From Account:			*	*	*	*	*	*	*	*	*	*	*	*
Checking			*		*						*	*	*	*
Savings				*		*	*	*	*	*				
From Account exists?			N	N	Y	Y	Y	Y	Y	Y	Y	Y	Y	Y
Amount of transfer:							*	*	*	*	*	*	*	*
zero							*				*			
more than in "from"								*				*		
takes "to" above maximum									*				*	
valid amount										*				*
Expected Results	"To Account Does Not Exist"		"From Account Does Not Exist"		"Cannot transfer from and to the same account."		"Cannot transfer zero."	"Insufficient funds in From Account. Re-enter or cancel."	"Cannot increase To Account above maximum."	Amount transferred between accounts.	"Cannot transfer zero."	"Insufficient funds in From Account. Re-enter or cancel."	"Cannot increase To Account above maximum."	Amount transferred between accounts.

Matrix ID:	**FW**									
Description:	**FAST Withdraw**									
Author:										
Original Release:	**1.0**			**Date:**	**######**					
Test case:	FW01	FW02	FW03	FW04	FW05	FW06	FW07	FW08	FW09	FW10
Control Points:										
From Account:	*	*	*	*	*	*	*	*	*	*
Checking	*		*	*	*	*				
Savings		*					*	*	*	*
From Account exists?	N	N	Y	Y	Y	Y	Y	Y	Y	Y
Amount of withdrawal:			*	*	*	*	*	*	*	*
zero			*				*			
more than in "from"				*				*		
Multiple of $20?					Y	Y			Y	Y
More than in FAST?					Y	N			Y	N
Expected Results	"From Account Does Not Exist"		"Cannot withdraw zero."	"Insufficient funds in From Account. Re-enter or cancel."	"Not enough cash to service your request. Re-enter or cancel."	Cash dispensed. Amount deducted from account.	"Cannot withdraw zero."	"Insufficient funds in From Account. Re-enter or cancel."	"Not enough cash to service your request. Re-enter or cancel."	Cash dispensed. Amount deducted from account.

Appendix F

Verification

Introduction

While it is not the intention of this book to go into depth on the subject of verification, it is a very important topic. In this appendix, we will give a short overview of the process. We sometimes call this process testing without testing.

Most of the time when we say testing, we mean something like "running the thing." So, how do we test without running the thing? How do we test without "testing"?

Let's take a closer look at our definition. The purpose of testing is to finds bugs, right? So if we expand our definition to include any activity intended to find bugs, then we go beyond just running the thing. We can include reviewing in our testing definition. Execution-based testing is called *validation*, and nonexecution-based testing is called *verification*.

Can we review code instead of executing it? Yes. Of course, most of our software is pretty complex, so reviewing it may not be all that efficient, but it is certainly worth a try.

Then, is reviewing code the best use of our time? That depends. It depends on where the bugs are that we're trying to find. Interestingly, industry averages tell us that 70 percent of the defects are actually in the requirements and design. So, if we can review things like requirements, specifications, designs, and the like, we can prevent possibly 70 percent or more of the defects before we even begin the "testing."

One of the problems with this, though, is that most people say, "We don't have time for all that stuff." This is a reasonable gut reaction, but the numbers don't bear this out. Actually, every time someone has tried to measure the resource and schedule impact of verification, they get the same result: **Projects are faster and cheaper if you do verification than if you don't.**

A variety of terms are in use to describe the process. Most commonly, we call this *peer review* or *technical review*. We'll use the general term, verification, in the section that follows.

Several levels of formality may be used. We'll discuss an overview of the most formal level; you can tailor this for your own needs. Consider the complexity of the work product, the risk if the final product fails, and the maturity of the organization and its tolerance for process. (There is a huge difference between process and procedures, but we won't go into that here.)

Let's look at the basics.

Verification is a process designed to identify — and thus eliminate — defects in all manner of work products. Examples of these work products include requirements, functional specifications, test plans, source code, user interface layouts, and others. The basic concept is that an ad hoc team comes together for the purpose of reviewing a work product. The author of the work product uses the review process to make sure that the product is as complete, clear, and correct as possible.

The members of the review team each play a specific assigned role. The roles are:

- **Author** — This role is self-assigned. This person is the one who created the work product in the first place.
- **Moderator** — This person has the responsibility to manage the entire review, and keep the meeting from

devolving into either a design session or a free-for-all! Not everybody wants this role, and not everybody who does want this role is suited for it.

- **Recorder** — This person takes the notes. This should *not* be the author or moderator.
- **Reviewers** — These are the folks who do the actual content review and present their findings.
- **[Observer]** — This is an optional addition to the team. The observer is usually there to learn how the process works so he or she can be prepared to take an active role in the future. We usually qualify this by saying that observers must have the moderator's permission to attend. Their role is to, as the name implies, observe, and not participate.
- **[Subject matter expert]** — This is an optional addition to the team. Sometimes it helps to have an additional member of the team who can clarify the matter at hand, and may also be able to help describe what is technically feasible.

There may be some overlap among the roles. For example, the moderator and the subject matter expert may also be reviewers. Note that for the author, there is no overlap: the author cannot fill any of the other roles.

There are eight steps in the process, as follows:

1. Planning
2. Kickoff
3. Individual Review
4. Collation / Discussion Preparation
5. Discussion
6. Defect Logging
7. Revision / Confirmation
8. Final Report

The following table shows who is involved at each of the steps.

	Author	Moderator	Recorder	Reviewers
Plan	✓	✓		
kickoff	✓	✓	✓	✓
Individual Review	(✓)	(✓)		✓
Collation	(✓)	✓		
Discussion	✓	✓	✓	✓
Defect Logging		(✓)	✓	
Revision, Confirmation	✓	(✓)		✓
Final Report	(✓)	✓		

Steps

Planning

Role	Action
Author	■ Select/request a moderator. ■ Assist moderator in his/her tasks.
Moderator	■ ·Assign roles. ■ Create review package. ■ Schedule meetings.

When an author determines that his or her work product is ready for review, he or she must first get someone to serve as moderator. The moderator functions as an overall coordinator of the review activities. In the planning stage, the moderator first assesses the readiness of the work product for review.

"Readiness" means there is a high likelihood of successful completion of the review. If the moderator determines that there are too many defects in the work product, for example, he or she may deem that the work product is not ready and suggest that the author clean it up before submitting the work product for verification.

Assuming readiness, the moderator selects individuals for the review team and assigns them their roles. The people chosen should represent the various stakeholders. Since almost all work products are responses to predecessor work products, one or more of the team members could be people who were responsible for the predecessor. Since almost all work products are the drivers for follow-on work, some of the team members could be people who must perform the next step or steps.

For example, consider the case of a product requirements document. This is the response to a marketing-requirements document, and therefore one member of the review team could be the author of the marketing-requirements document. This allows for assurance that the product-requirements document correctly interprets the marketing requirements. Similarly, the product-requirements document is input to the functional design description and the test plan, so team members could include both the person who will create the functional design description and the person who will create the test plan.

Generally, one should avoid having as a team member any manager who has his or her own employees on the review team. It is occasionally necessary to ignore this rule, but one should do so with caution. Some people are less comfortable in this situation than others.

The ideal size for the review team is five to nine people.

The review package consists of the work product, any predecessor documents, and the standard for the type of article. The package may be hard copy, soft copy, or merely pointers to where the information exists.

Kickoff

Role	Action
Moderator	■ Distribute review package. ■ Conduct meeting. ■ Secure commitments.
Author	■ Present high-level overview of the items to be reviewed.
Reviewers	■ Listen and learn. ■ Ask questions.
Recorder	■ Log duration of the meeting. ■ Log list of attendees.

At the kickoff meeting, the team gets information about the work product. If the review package is hard copy, it is distributed at this meeting. Because the team may be scattered across several locations, the material must be available for all team members at this time.

The kickoff meeting is intended to be quite brief. It generally lasts no more than 30 minutes. At the meeting, the author will give a brief summary of the article, and may alert the team to areas of concern. It may also happen that some areas of the article are not completed, and so the author would point this out. Those areas may be subject for review at a later date.

The kickoff should be at least five working days prior to the discussion for the reviewers to have sufficient time for their individual review. This allows the reviewers the flexibility to weave their preparation around their primary assignments. As an alternative, the team may decide how long they need and schedule the discussion as a result of that decision at the kickoff.

If any reviewers feel that they cannot complete the individual review in the allotted time, this is their opportunity to either opt for replacement or suggest a different date for the discussion.

The moderator should remind the team members of the purpose of the technical review. The purpose is to develop findings for the work product, not to redesign the article.

The recorder's function here is to log the number of attendees and the duration of the meeting. This information will be useful later when we are calculating the return-on-investment (ROI) of the process.

Note that the kickoff meeting does not necessarily need to be a face-to-face gathering. In fact, it may be that team members are in different locations. Consider conference calls and video hook-ups. In some circumstances, email might also be considered as an alternative. There are some disadvantages to this, but it may occasionally be necessary.

Individual Review

Role	Action
Reviewers	■ Review the article. ■ Record findings. ■ Transmit findings to the moderator before the discussion.
Moderator	■ Monitor reviewers' progress. ■ Help reviewers with process issues.
Author	■ Answer questions from the reviewers.

During this step, the reviewers perform their individual review and gather their findings. The findings belong in one of the following categories:

- Defects
- Questions
- External issues

- Praise

Using discrete categories helps assure that the review does not devolve into a redesign exercise. The category list may be upgraded or modified from time to time, but not on a product-by-product basis. This will allow for project comparisons and statistical analyses.

Defects

The defects fall into one of five types:

- **Error** — A statement is incorrect.
- **Conflict** — A statement is in disagreement with a different statement in the work product.
- **Missing** — Some necessary or required information is not present.
- **Extra** — Some feature or design has been added that is not accounted for in the predecessor document. For example, if there is no requirement for a particular product to run on some platform, then having a specification or design to support that platform would be a defect of type "extra."
- **Unclear** — A statement in the work product has several possible interpretations or is written in a way that could confuse the user of the article.

It should be noted that the defects identified during Individual Review are not recorded in the Incident Management database at this time. That action occurs after the discussion, after consensus has been reached that the finding is, in fact, a defect.

Questions

Some findings are questions to be asked of either the author or subject matter expert. Generally, these are requests for background information or information that is nominally outside the area of the work product. One word of caution: if a reviewer has a question, it may be that something is missing or unclear. Either of these situations would be a defect, not a question.

External Issues

Sometimes, reviewers uncover difficulties that are relevant to the use of the product being developed, but not under the control of the team doing the developing. For example, if a specification calls for use of a third-party application, a potential External Issue could concern run-time licenses for that application.

Praise

It is useful to take note of things that are done especially well in the work product, so that others may learn. Besides, many authors feel a bit sensitive about having their work scrutinized, and it's nice to complement them. Of course, the goal is to conduct the reviews in such a way that no one feels picked on, but as the process is introduced, there may be a bit of trepidation.

The reviewers transmit their findings to the moderator the day before the discussion. Any errors such as typos, grammatical errors, spelling errors, and the like should be sent separately from the findings. These will be handed over to the author and not covered in the meeting. (Some people just like to use marked-up copies of the article for this purpose.)

Collation

Role	Action
Moderator	■ Gather findings. ■ Prepare agenda.
Author	■ Assist moderator.

The moderator collects the findings and prepares the agenda for the meeting. Most moderators choose to handle the findings in page sequence rather than skipping all around in the work product. Occasionally, there may be reasons for placing a particularly serious problem first regardless of its location.

If many defects are being reported, the moderator should consider canceling the review, since the work product may not be quite ready. In this situation, the findings should be given to the author for use in updating the article. A review can then be rescheduled.

Discussion

Role	Action
Moderator	■ Keep discussion focused on identification, not solution. ■ Keep discussion focused on the work product, not the author.
Reviewers	■ Present findings. ■ Participate in determining review result.
Recorder	■ Log prep time for each reviewer. ■ Finalize the findings log. ■ Summarize findings at end of discussion. ■ Log duration and attendees.
Author	■ Listen and learn. ■ Answer questions if asked. ■ Thank the reviewers for their help.
Observer	■ Observe.
Manager	■ Stay away.

A suggested agenda is:

- Moderator distributes copies of agenda and collation report to reviewers.

- Moderator describes purpose of meeting, process, and ground rules.
- Moderator polls reviewers, asking how much time they spent in their preparation. If any of the reviewers are not prepared, they should change role from reviewer to observer if they wish to remain. If too many reviewers are not prepared, the meeting should be rescheduled for another time.
- Moderator polls reviewers for any general comments before beginning a point-by-point review. This may include general praise or comments about missing items that cannot be pegged to a particular location in the work product.
- Each of the identified findings is presented in sequence. If any of the findings is a question, the team decides if this indicates a defect or not. If it is not a defect, the author answers the question. For findings of type defect, consensus is reached on the severity and type.
- Group searches for new defects. These would be findings not previously reported. Typically, the earlier discussion may trigger observations in the team that no one individual had reported.
- Recorder notes any new findings as well as changes to the previously identified findings. This includes the description, severity, and type. The severities are:
    1. The end product would be unusable if this were not fixed.
    2. A major function of the end product would be unusable if this were not fixed.
    3. A feature (part of a function) of the end product would be unusable if this were not fixed.
    4. A particular situation would cause a failure in the end product if this were not fixed.

5. This would not necessarily result in an observable failure in the end product, but could potentially cause some difficulty or annoyance.

- Recorder reads the list of findings. This gives the person who reported it a chance to add clarification if necessary, and gives the author a chance to ask any final questions about it. It also gives the team a chance to hear the entire list, which is useful if forming an overall impression. This helps with the determination of the discussion outcome.
- Team determines the outcome. Four possible outcomes are:
    - **Accept as is** — No changes are necessary.
    - **Accept with changes** — Author makes the changes based on the findings. No confirmation is necessary.
    - **Revise with informal confirmation** — Author makes changes based on the findings. The changes are informally confirmed.
    - **Revise and hold another formal review** — The findings are significant enough that the team decides that another Formal Review is needed after the author has made the changes.
- If the outcome was "Revise with informal confirmation," the team decides on the confirmation technique(s), as well as assigning individuals to the confirmation as appropriate. Examples of informal confirmation techniques are:
    - One person from the review team confirms (no meeting).
    - Several people from the team confirm (no meeting).
    - Author presents changes to team (meeting).
- Author collects any marked packages that may contain the typos, etc., if they have not been previously transmitted.

- Author thanks the team members.

The discussion should last no more than two hours. It is sometimes necessary to divide an article into sections to achieve this goal. Rarely, an article is long, complex, and cannot be divided. In this case, the meeting may have to exceed the two-hour limit.

Defect Logging

Role	Action
Recorder	■ Log defects to the incident management database.

Following the discussion, the recorder enters the defects into the incident management system. This is not the onerous chore it may seem to be, for two reasons. First, because most of the defects will have been transmitted electronically, cut-and-paste can be used. Second, the expectation is that the number of defects found will not be prohibitive, or the discussion would not have taken place. As an alternative, some review teams may choose to use a less formal method of tracking the defects, such as a spreadsheet. (On the other hand, if you are going to copy the information to a spreadsheet, why not just go ahead and copy it to the incident manager so you can take advantage of the tools available?)

Revision, Confirmation

Role	Action
Author	■ Revise the work product as indicated by the review findings.
Moderator	■ Monitor revision progress. ■ Assure all revisions have been made.
Reviewers	■ Confirm revisions as assigned during the discussion.

Final Report

Role	Action
Moderator	■ Summarize the verification. ■ Perform statistical analysis as needed. ■ Make recommendations as appropriate.

The statistical analysis addresses issues such as number of findings of each type and how much time on average was spent per finding.

References

Chapter 1

Ohno, Taiichi. *The Toyota Production System* ISBN 0-915299-14-3.

Standish Group International, Inc. *CHAOS Report*.

National Institute of Science and Technology (NIST). 2002 study.

Cartoons courtesy of Corporate Solutions Consulting (UK) Limited.

Boehm, B. and Basili, V. "Software Defect Reduction Top 10 List," *IEEE Computer*, IEEE Computer Society, Vol. 34, No. 1, January 2001, pp. 135-137.

Chapter 2

United States National Institute of Standards and Technology.

Fagan, Michael. www.mfagan.com.

NASA, *Software Formal Inspections Guidebook*, NASA-GB-A302.

Robertson, James and Robertson, Suzanne. *Mastering the Requirements Process*.

Chapter 5

Juran, J.M., *Quality Control Handbook.*

Giga Information Group 2001, *Justifying IT Investments: Quality Assurance.*

Chapter 6

Six Sigma, Motorola, Inc.

Chapter 7

Capability Maturity Model Integration (CMMI), Carnegie Mellon University.

About the Authors

Andreas Golze, Global Practice Director of Mercury's Professional Services, is an expert with many years' experience in the IT industry. He is one of the founders of the Mercury Quality Model (MQM), which is now the standard for many large-scale enterprise organizations around the globe. Before his move to Mercury, Andreas served as the Senior Executive at the TestLab Business Unit of SQS AG, having earlier crafted and built up this unit in the role of Department Manager. He was also responsible for developing and expanding partner business. Andreas Golze studied computer science and minored in business studies at the University of the Armed Forces in Munich. His career began with a position as a programming officer at NATO in Belgium. Today, Mr. Golze lives in Cologne, Germany with his wife, Petra and their four children.

Charlie Li, Director of Product Marketing for Application Delivery Solutions at Mercury Interactive, has extensive experience consulting with Fortune 500 customers on large-scale quality management and testing projects in his seven years with Mercury. Previously, he served as the Practice Director of Mercury's Professional Services and is one of the founders of the Mercury Quality Model, which is now the standard for many large-scale enterprise organizations around the globe. Charlie has also built relationships and is working closely with partners like SAP, WIPRO, and Infosys, which are driving quality innovations into new markets. Charlie started his career as an IT consultant and software engineer and holds a computer science degree from the Georgia Institute of Technology. Today, Mr. Li lives in Atlanta, Georgia with his wife, Mandy and their dog Lucy.

Shel Prince, Principle Process Consultant of Mercury's Professional Services, has been in the software quality field for almost 40 years, entering the workforce after undergraduate study in Physics and graduate studies in Business and Psychology. As one of the co-founders of the Mercury Quality Model, Shel has leveraged his vast experience in the quality field to continuously innovate the quality model. Prior to joining Mercury, he was a consultant for large-scale enterprise companies and governments in many parts of the world. His broad range of experience helped in forming his theories and approach to the fields of software quality and software testing. Today, Mr. Prince lives in Sammamish, Washington with his wife, Nancy and their dog Beau.